PACTS & TREATIES

INDIAN TREATIES

SUSAN DUDLEY GOLD

TWENTY-FIRST CENTURY BOOKS
A Division of Henry Holt and Company
New York

To Abigail Libby, who taught her students to love history and showed them how to search for the truth

Twenty-First Century Books
A Division of Henry Holt and Company, Inc.
115 West 18th Street
New York, NY 10011

Henry Holt® and colophon are trademarks of
Henry Holt and Company, Inc.
Publishers since 1866

Published in Canada by Fitzhenry & Whiteside Ltd.
195 Allstate Parkway, Markham, Ontario, L3R 4T8

Library of Congress Cataloging-in-Publication Data
Gold, Susan Dudley
Indian treaties / Susan Dudley Gold. — 1st ed.
p. cm. — (Pacts & treaties)
Includes bibliographical references and index.
Summary: Describes the numerous treaties between the various Native American peoples and the settlers from Europe and explains how these new inhabitants used ways unfamiliar to the Indians to take their lands.
1. Indians of North America—Treaties—Juvenile literature. 2. Indians of North America—Government relations—Juvenile literature. [1. Indians of North America—Treaties. 2. Indians of North America—Government relations.
I. Title. I. Series.
E95.G65   1997
323.1'197073—dc21   96–47621
                                                                        CIP
                                                                        AC

Photo Credits
Cover illustration and illustrations on pages 10, 20, 44, and 62 © 1996 North Wind Picture Archives.
Illustrations on pages 4, 18, 64, 88, and 101 provided by North Wind Picture Archives.
Illustration on page 83 provided by Woolaroc Museum, Bartlesville, Oklahoma.
Illustrations on pages 59, 67, and 90 provided by the Library of Congress.
Illustration on page 32 provided by Stock Montage.
Illustration on page 112 provided by Bettmann.
Maps on pages 15, 23, 26, 29, 36, 38, 42, 47, 53, 65, 69, 72, 75, 78, 95, 98, 103, 107, 110, and 115 © 1996 Susan D. Gold.

Design, Typesetting, and Layout
Custom Communications

ISBN 0-8050-4813-8
First Edition 1997

Printed in the United States of America
All first editions are printed on acid-free paper ∞.
10 9 8 7 6 5 4 3 2 1

CONTENTS

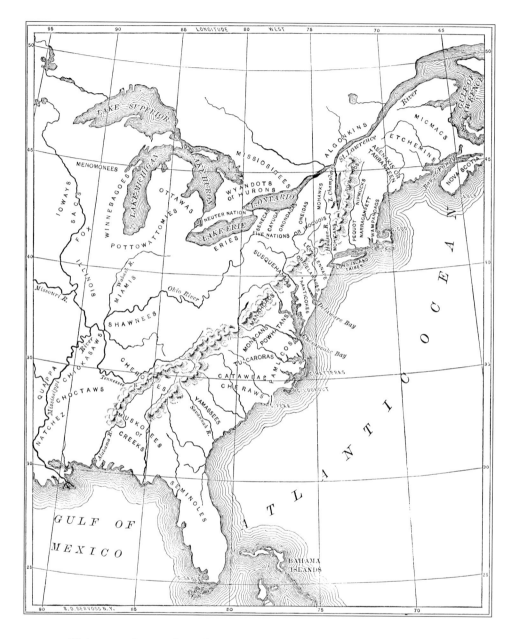

This map shows where the major Indian tribes lived when the Pilgrims arrived in America.

Introduction

You Cannot Sell a Country

Native Americans signed their first treaties granting land to English colonists in the 1600s. From that time until 1871 when the Congress of the United States decreed that Indians could no longer issue treaties, the native tribes made hundreds of pacts with the settlers who had invaded their lands.

The treaties guaranteed the Indians peace, European goods and supplies, money, and land reserved for them alone. In return, the Indian nations turned over millions of acres to the land-hungry settlers until, finally, there was no more land to sell and nowhere for the Indians to call home. By 1947, when Congress claimed ownership of Alaska's valuable land and water resources, the tribes of North America had lost nearly two billion acres of land, in many cases for a penny or less an acre. They signed 372 treaties with the Americans, many more with the English before them.

Though the Pilgrims knew that Indians existed in the New World, they considered the territory available to those hardy English souls who first settled there. The entire continent, they contended, had been claimed by British explorers in the name of the Crown. Where Indians occupied prized land, colonists stood ready to barter with goods and cash and seal the deal with treaties written in the King's English.

On paper, many of the treaties may have sounded reasonable, at least to the Europeans: they were buying land in exchange for cash and other benefits. The problem was that treaties were never part of Indian culture. The native tribes settled disputes through warfare, through councils, and through ancient rituals. They had no written language, no books, no official records. Their rich cultural history was preserved in storytelling, not in written words. They understood little of the concept of treaties or of what was written in them.

Red Cloud (Mahpiua Luta), the Oglala chief who signed a peace treaty in 1868 after forcing the U.S. government to stop building forts in Indian country, described how the Americans tricked him:

> In 1868 men came out and brought papers. We could not read them, and they did not tell us truly what was in them. . . . When I reached Washington the Great Father [President Grant] explained to me what the treaty was, and showed me that the interpreters had deceived me.[1]

In Europe, a man's worth and wealth were determined by how much land he owned. The Indians had no concept of individual land ownership. No one Indian owned property. The tribe as a whole used the land to survive, either for farming or for hunting grounds. They viewed the treaties they signed with the English and later the Americans as leases that allowed settlers to live on the land, farm it, walk over the land, and use its waters and its wildlife. When the settlers had finished with the land, the Indians surmised, the tribe would once again put it to use.

"Sell a country!" Shawnee chief Tecumseh had said, aghast at the idea. "Why not sell the air, the clouds and the great sea, as well as the earth? Did not the Great Spirit make them all for the use of his children?"[2]

No one chief had the right to sign treaties for the tribe. Elders met as a council to guide and to direct the chief, who consulted young men in the tribe and women as well before taking action.

Unscrupulous land speculators, eager to expand their holdings, bribed individual chiefs and persuaded them to sign treaties that gave away tribal lands. When members of the tribe protested, the people who had settled on the land almost always refused to give it up. The Indians then had to choose between leaving their homes or fighting to remain there.

Though the Europeans and the Americans wrote the treaties, it was they who most often broke the written agreements. Indians pledged to give up large portions of the land they controlled in exchange for peace and a small plot set aside for their exclusive use. It wasn't long, however, before settlers began trespassing on the Indian reserve. Settlers paid little attention to the natives' claims to the land. Claiming the best land they could find, the settlers disregarded treaty terms negotiated by their government. Often, that meant settling on Indian land.

Many settlers bought their land from speculators, who offered no proof that they owned the property but sold it anyway—at astonishing profits. Still others, known as squatters, simply camped out on lands, claiming them as their own. In both cases, the land was often located on Indian reserves.

Word spread quickly that wealth and cheap land awaited in America. By 1662, New England was home to forty thousand colonists, twice the number of Indians in the area. Outnumbered and overpowered by superior weapons, Indians were often forced to sign unfavorable treaties or die. When they fought against outrageous treaty terms, they usually lost even more land after their inevitable defeat.

Chief Joseph, leader of the Nez Percé Indians of Oregon, told Congress in 1877 how his tribe had been cheated out of their land by the government. Despite his eloquence, Chief Joseph was held captive and later died on a reservation in Washington without ever seeing his homeland again.

Chief Joseph's speech ended with a story that summed up his people's experience with American treaties:

> Suppose a white man should come to me and say, "Joseph, I like your horses, and I want to buy them." I say to him, "No, my horses suit me, I will not sell them." Then he goes to my neighbor, and says to him: "Joseph has some good horses. I want to buy them, but he refuses to sell." My neigh-

bor answers, "Pay me the money, and I will sell you Joseph's horses." The white man returns to me, and says, "Joseph, I have bought your horses, and you must let me have them." If we sold our lands to the Government, this is the way they were bought.[3]

Today, nearly two million Indians, including Eskimos and Aleuts, live in the United States. A little less than one-quarter of them live on land reserved for them by the U.S. government. Many have left their tribes to live in cities and towns across America.

Their battle to reclaim their identity as separate nations continues today, not on the warpath but in the courts. In many cases, native peoples are using the treaties signed by their chiefs a century ago to plead their cause. They point to these written litanies of broken promises and treacherous deceit, and they demand justice.

Indians speaking English greeted the Pilgrims of Massachusetts Bay Colony.

One

New England

Crowded aboard their tiny vessels, peering into the mist and fog, the British Pilgrims at last saw what they sought: land. Unlike the adventurers before them who lusted after gold, the strong-willed Pilgrims wanted a home, a place they could call their own.

But this land they claimed for themselves, in 1620, already belonged to others. These first Americans—whom Christopher Columbus had dubbed Indians in the mistaken notion that the continent he discovered had been India—numbered in the millions. It is estimated that in 1492 from ten million to fifteen million natives lived in North America, mainly along the coasts and the fertile river valleys. Their villages stretched across the continent, each tribe individual in its language, customs, dress, and lifestyle. They spoke 550 different languages or dialects and practiced complex religions that governed the lives of all tribe members. The natives lived in tribal communes, where everyone shared food, wealth, and work.

Where the land was fertile, tribes settled in villages and grew corn, tomatoes, and other crops. They supplemented their diet with wild deer and smaller animals found in the hunting grounds near their villages. On the plains, natives hunted buffalo. Farther west, along the Pacific coast, tribes wandered from place to place, gathering wild plants for food. The earliest tribes had probably lived in these lands for fifteen thousand years.

Land, according to Indian culture, could not be owned by humans. Humans died, moved on; land remained. Although Indians dismissed the notion of owning land, the tribe claimed the right to control the use of the land its people needed to survive. The tribe's members drove other tribes from the land used by their ancestors. Individuals, however, including chiefs, controlled no land.

Spanish, French, Dutch, and English explorers and traders brought death and disease to the native people. The Indians had never been exposed to smallpox and other European diseases and, therefore, had no immunity to them. When epidemics broke out, millions died. By the time English settlers arrived in America in the 1600s, less than one-fifth of the population—about two million—survived.

When the Pilgrims landed at Plymouth Rock in 1620, they saw no one living on the land they claimed. William Bradford, who recorded his experiences as a member of the early settlers, noted: "There is neither man, woman, nor child remaining, as indeed we have found none, so that there is none to hinder our possession or to lay claim unto it."[1]

The territory, however, lay in the midst of a widespread nation, the Wampanoag Confederacy, consisting of eight large villages and thirty smaller ones stretching from the eastern shore of Narragansett Bay to Cape Cod. It was ruled by Usamequin, also known as Massasoit.

The Pilgrims, seeking refuge from the December winter of 1620, had landed at the site of the deserted village of Patuxet. They called their new colony Plimouth (later to be called Plymouth). Three years before, Patuxet—on the shore of Cape Cod Bay—had been a thriving Wampanoag village. There, natives had raised corn, fertilized with the fish they caught in the ocean, and had hunted the plentiful deer that grazed in the nearby fields. A plague had changed the peaceful lives of the villagers. The deadly disease, carried to the natives by European traders, had killed every man, woman, and child in the village.

The Indians of the Wampanoag tribe no doubt kept a close watch on their new neighbors that first winter. But it was not until the following March that they made themselves known to the settlers. Samoset, a member of the Abenaki tribe who was visiting the Wampanoags, was the first to greet the newcomers. Tall and regal in his headdress, Samoset stepped from the forest and addressed the startled Pilgrims in English.

"Welcome, Englishmen," he said. He had learned the language from traders who visited his tribe on the Maine coast. Later, he introduced the Pilgrims to Squanto, who also spoke to them in their own language. Squanto had been kidnapped by an English sea captain in 1614 and had learned the English language and the ways of Europeans before making his way back to his homeland. The two English-speaking Indians interpreted for Massasoit and the sixty warriors he brought to meet the settlers.

Massasoit, leader of the Wampanoag Confederacy, saw the advantages of an alliance with this new tribe of men with their deadly guns. The plague that had destroyed Patuxet had wiped out many members of his tribe. The powerful Narragansetts, from their base on the other side of the bay, had begun to threaten Massasoit's tribe.

In a formal ceremony after sharing a meal, Massasoit signed a peace treaty with Plymouth Governor John Carver in 1621. In it, both the colonists and the Indians pledged to protect each other from attack.

It proved to be the first of many treaties Massasoit signed with the settlers. With the help of Squanto and other Indians, the Pilgrims learned to plant corn and to hunt deer, wild turkey, and the twelve-foot-long sturgeon that the Indians killed with an ax. The Pilgrims also learned to harvest the oysters that grew thirteen inches across in Cape Cod Bay and to shoot ducks, so plentiful they blackened the sky as they flew to nesting sites along the Massachusetts shore. Both Indians and settlers marked the first Thanksgiving together in a jubilant, three-day celebration of games, feasts, and friendship.

As Plymouth Colony thrived, more English settlers sailed into Cape Cod, eager to establish their own colonies. The alliance between the Wampanoags and the settlers held for more than forty years, but only because the Indians agreed to sign over portions of their land to the new arrivals.

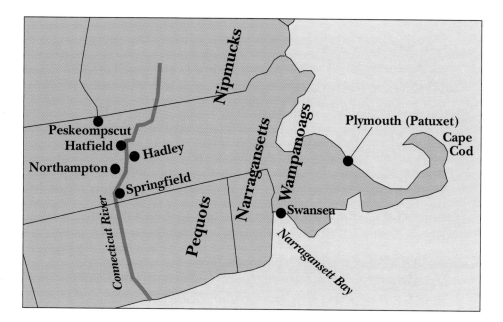

The Wampanoag Confederacy occupied much of the eastern Massachusetts shoreline from Cape Cod to Narragansett Bay.

During that time, the Wampanoags regained their strength against the Narragansett tribe. But by the time Massasoit died in 1662, it was the settlers, not an enemy Indian tribe, that threatened to overrun Wampanoag lands and way of life. Some forty thousand colonists had taken over prime hunting grounds in New England. Those Indians unable to kill enough deer to survive were forced to work for the settlers as servants and laborers in the fields. Indians in the weaker tribes lived on reserves set aside for them. They were forbidden to fish or hunt on Sundays. So-called praying Indians—those who had converted to Christianity—were secluded in their own villages, away from the influence of the tribe.

Massasoit's oldest son, Wamsutta (whom the Puritans called Alexander), became chief after his father's death. The Puritans at Plymouth detained and questioned the young chief. The tribe's resentment overflowed when Wamsutta became sick and died shortly after the Puritans released him. His tribe believed he had been poisoned by his captors.

KING PHILIP'S WAR

Metacom, Massasoit's younger son, took over leadership of the tribe. The Puritans called him King Philip and considered him a troublemaker. Several times they brought him to Plymouth to question him. A skilled orator, Metacom reassured them all was well. Once released, however, he worked to unite surrounding tribes against the colonists.

In 1671, the colonists passed a decree that banned the possession of firearms by the Wampanoags. Metacom resisted, knowing his people would starve without guns. The tribe had learned to use guns from European traders and now were dependent on the guns to kill the game they ate. Metacom tried to win support from the powerful Narragansetts and Nipmucks, rival tribes in the area. When he failed, the chief was forced to sign a treaty with the Puritans giving up the tribe's guns, promising to pay an annual fee of one hundred pounds to the settlers, and pledging to live in peace. A clause in the treaty warned that Metacom "must expect to smart for it" if he opposed the English settlers.[2]

In 1675, an Indian who worked for the Puritans as an

informer was murdered. The Puritans blamed the Wampanoags and hung three of their warriors. Furious at what they considered interference in tribal matters, a group of young warriors attacked Swansea, a Puritan town, on June 20, 1675. During a three-day rampage, they killed cattle and terrorized the inhabitants. During the fracas, a young colonist shot and wounded one of the Indians.

That was all the tribes needed to declare war. They set fire to four outlying towns. By this time, several Massachusetts tribes, including the mighty Nipmucks, had joined forces with the Wampanoags under Metacom's leadership. As the Indians won more and more victories, the war reached into Maine, where other tribes took up their weapons against the English settlers.

Colonial men and boys soon formed a militia to protect their homes from Indian warriors. Fighting guerrilla-style, the Indians hid in the autumn foliage and attacked the passing colonial troops. South of Deerfield, they attacked a wagon train filled with crops harvested from farms along the Connecticut Valley. The crops were destroyed, and all but two of the sixty men guarding the wagons were killed. As town after town burned, it looked as if the tribes might win the war, known as King Philip's War. Warriors attacked Hadley, Northampton, Hatfield, and Springfield. Terrified Massachusetts inhabitants reported that Indian warriors waited outside their towns "like the lightning on the edge of clouds."[3]

The Narragansetts, longtime foes of the Wampanoags, joined the fray after Massachusetts soldiers slaughtered six hundred native men, women, and children in their Rhode Island settlement in December 1675. Land

Metacom was killed by an Indian hired by the Puritans.

speculators used the opportunity to take over much of the fertile lands along Narragansett Bay.

As winter slipped into spring, the war began to change course. The well-armed New England militia of one thousand men attacked a sleeping Wampanoag camp in 1676 and seized three hundred of Metacom's followers. The soldiers killed or sold the captives into slavery, then burned the tribe's villages and crops. In April, the colonists killed Narragansett leader, Canonchet. His head, cut from his body, was sent to Hartford, where colonial leaders could view it.

With help from praying Indians, the New England forces captured the Indian village of Peskeompscut and burned the tribe's crops throughout the valley. The starving Indians retreated to the wilds of New Hampshire as the colonial army pledged to "exterminate the rabid animals."[4] In August, the colonists reached Metacom's camp and captured or killed 173 Indians. Many of the captives, including Metacom's wife and nine-year-old son, were sold as slaves in the Caribbean.

DEATH OF METACOM

In despair, the Indian leader returned to the village of his birth. On August 12, 1676, the New England forces tracked Metacom to Assowomset Swamp. There, an Indian hired by the colonists shot him through the heart. The Puritans cut off his head and stuck it on a post in Plymouth, where it stayed for twenty years, a gory symbol of the Indian nation's defeat. Little more than half a century had passed since Metacom's father had so joyfully celebrated his tribe's friendship with the English settlers who had claimed this land as their own.

The war raged for one and one-half years more as tribes in Maine and New Hampshire raided English settlements. Eventually, colonial soldiers tracked down the remaining Indian rebels and killed or enslaved them.

Fifty-two of the ninety English settlements in New England had been damaged in the war; six hundred colonial men, women, and children had been killed; twelve hundred homes were destroyed.[5]

The Indians suffered far greater losses. Three thousand of their people lay dead; hundreds more were sold as slaves. Several of the smaller tribes were wiped out completely. The once-mighty tribes of New England were no more.

In 1682, the Delawares sold land to William Penn. Both sides pledged to live in friendship forever.

Two

Land Grabs and Rebellion

Early on the morning of September 9, 1737, three men lined up along the west bank of the Delaware River. The fastest runners in the area, they had been handpicked by Pennsylvania officials. The three woodsmen, Edward Marshall, James Yeates, and Solomon Jennings, had trained hard for the past nine days for the marathon that was about to take place. The man who walked the farthest had been promised five pounds sterling and five hundred acres of land.

As soon as the sun rose, they would begin the walk along the river. All the land they covered in the next eighteen hours would become the property of the Pennsylvania province. The land would then be opened to settlers, eager to build homes in the fertile river valley.

Some of the would-be settlers stood along the river, ready to cheer on the woodsmen. Beside them, members of the Lenni Lenape tribe (or Delawares, as they were called by the settlers in Pennsylvania) waited to see how much land they would have to turn over to their colonial neighbors.

The marathon was part of the terms of a land treaty known as the Walking Purchase. It was based on a 1686 treaty signed by Delaware chiefs and William Penn, founder of Pennsylvania. Quaker leader Penn was so well respected among the Indians for his fairness and honesty that, according to legend, Indians who wished to pay a compliment to a colonist said he was "like William Penn."[1]

Penn was one colonist who understood the tribal structure. He tried to get permission from all tribes involved before concluding treaties to buy land in the Pennsylvania region. In the treaty of July 15, 1682, the first in which the Delaware chiefs sold land to Penn, both sides pledged to live as friends as long as the sun and moon shall shine. "We are met on the broad pathway of good faith and good will," the treaty read, "so that no advantage is to be taken on either side, but all to be openness, brotherhood, and love."[2]

The 1686 deed negotiated by Penn described the northern boundary of land purchased as being "as far as a Man can go in one Day and a half [eighteen hours]."[3] For fifty years, the boundary had never been walked.

When William Penn died, his thirty-five-year-old son, Thomas Penn, took over the management of Pennsylvania. With an increasing number of settlers moving into the area, disputes began to arise over the exact boundary of the property referred to in the Walking Purchase. To settle the matter, Thomas Penn, his brother John, and other officials met with the Delaware chiefs at a council in 1734. The chiefs agreed that the deed was legal and

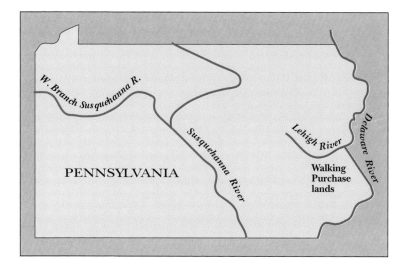

Delaware Indians lost 1,200 square miles of land along the Delaware River as a result of the Walking Purchase.

signed the Walking Purchase treaty in 1737 stipulating that the walk should take place to determine the boundary once and for all. They assumed that the land in question would account for only a small portion of the property their tribe had occupied for centuries.

The crowd's excitement mounted as the walk began. The three men soon broke into a loping gait. Delaware observers along the trail protested that the deed required the men to walk, not run, the course. Their protests seemed to spur the men to race even faster.

The Indians also objected to the course itself. All along the way, a path had been cut through the underbrush to speed the walkers' passage. Horses waited along the course to carry the walkers quickly across rivers and streams that blocked their way.

As the long day wore on, the runners stopped for food and water provided for them by the race organizers. Finally, as the sun set, only one man remained in the race. At the end of eighteen hours, he jogged past the observers in one last spurt of energy, then collapsed on the trail. He had reached all the way to the fork of the Lehigh and Delaware rivers, a distance of sixty-five miles. With the northern boundary established, the parcel of land ceded by the Delawares amounted to twelve hundred square miles, double the amount envisioned by the tribe.

The Delawares charged fraud and refused to leave their lands. Thomas Penn, insisting that the terms of the deed had been fulfilled legally, convinced the Iroquois tribes to force the weaker Delawares off the property. The dispossessed tribe settled along the Susquehanna River and eventually joined forces with the French against the British.

At a treaty conference in Easton, Pennsylvania, almost twenty years later, Chief Teedyuscung, known as King of the Delawares, bitterly described the deceit that deprived his tribe of their ancestral lands:

> This very ground that is under me was my land and inheritance, and is taken from me by fraud. . . . When I had agreed to sell the land to the old Proprietary [William Penn], by the course of the river, the young Proprietaries [Thomas and John Penn] came, and got it run by a straight course, by the compass, and by that means took in double the quantity intended to be sold.[4]

By 1754, battles between the French traders and the English settlers along the Ohio River valley and the Great Lakes regions had developed into a full-fledged war between England and France in Europe. The war between England and France in Europe was dubbed the Seven Years' War. In America, the war was called the French and Indian War because of the involvement of Indian tribes in the fighting.

Throughout the end of the 1600s and into the mid-1700s, control of the area had teetered between the French and the English. The Indians preferred to stay out of the conflict as much as possible. When they did pledge allegiance, it was in return for promises the tribes would be protected or in revenge for actions taken against the Indians by the other side.

Aware of the value of Indian allies, both the English and the French made an effort to remain on good terms with the tribes. Delegations of Indian chiefs were wined and dined in France and England in a bid to win the support of their tribes.

The majority of the Iroquois nations—Cayugas, Mohawks, Oneidas, Onondagas, Senecas, and Tuscaroras—remained loyal to the British; the French received help from the Ottawas, Ojibwas, Miamis, Potawatomis, Menominees, Shawnees, Hurons, Delawares, Abenakis, Nipissings, and Algonquins.

The Treaty of Paris ended the French and Indian War in 1763. Under the treaty's terms, France ceded to England all its land east of the Mississippi River except New

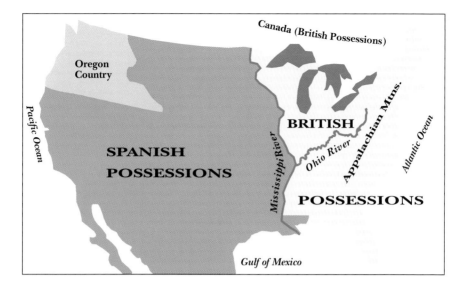

The treaty signed at the end of the French and Indian War gave England control of most of the lands east of the Mississippi River.

Orleans and two small islands in St. Lawrence Bay. France gave New Orleans and its lands west of the Mississippi to Spain as a reward for that country's help during the Seven Years' War. No mention was made of the Indians' claim to the lands along the Mississippi or of their service as warriors for both European countries.

PONTIAC'S REBELLION

The end of the French and Indian War had a drastic effect on the Indians' power in the region. Without the French threat, the English no longer needed help from Indian allies. The tribes were now at the mercy of the English. The situation was particularly grim for the tribes that had sided with the French.

The Indians were also worried about the opening of the fertile lands between the Appalachians and the Ohio River. Much of the land had been previously controlled by the French, who established trading posts but had not settled the territory. The English colonists, however, were poised to rush onto the lands and build homes there.

A few English leaders, foreseeing the problems a land grab would cause between settlers and the Indians, tried to avert disaster. The Board of Trade, based in England, appointed two superintendents to oversee the Indian tribes in America: Sir William Johnson in the north and Edmund Atkin in the south. The board also sought to control the traders doing business with the Indians.

The Earl of Shelburne, who served as president of the Board of Trade and later became England's prime minister, proposed a plan that would ban settlers west of the Appalachians. Under the plan, the territory would be set aside for the Indians, protecting them, at least temporarily, from the promised onslaught of settlers.

Others, however, had little sympathy for or understanding of the Indians. Sir Jeffrey Amherst, who as commander of the British army was in charge of Indian affairs in America for England, exhibited a haughty disdain for the tribes, even those who had fought for his side in the war. He referred to Indians as "the vilest race of beings that ever infested the earth"[5] and abruptly ordered an end to the French practice of giving guns and ammunition to the Indians for their hunting parties. As a sign of goodwill, the French had also given Indians food and clothing when their supplies ran short. This practice, too, was discontinued by Amherst.

The English commander's actions infuriated Ottawa chief Pontiac, whose people lived near Detroit. Pontiac had led the western and Great Lakes tribes against the English during the French and Indian War. He hated the English and feared the settlers would push his tribe off their lands.

Inspired by a Delaware prophet named Neolin who preached that Indians should return to traditional ways of life, Pontiac convinced the tribes of the Great Lakes and Ohio regions to join forces against the settlers. Uniting with the forty-year-old chief's Ottawa tribe were the Chippewas, Potawatomis, Menominees, Hurons, Delawares, Shawnees, Senecas, Fox, Mingos, Kickapoos, Mascoutens, Weas, Sauk, and Miamis. The French traders still in the area were eager to see an Indian rebellion against their old enemy, the English. They urged the tribes on, promising French aid to the warring tribes.

On May 7, 1763, Pontiac and his forces approached Fort Detroit, but they were no match for the well-armed British troops, who had been warned by a Chippewa girl of the pending attack. Thwarted, the Indians left and returned later with more warriors, who surrounded the fort and began a long siege that lasted for the next five months. At the same time, warriors of the Delaware, Mingo, Shawnee, Chippewa, Seneca, Kickapoo, Miami, and other tribes lay siege to Fort Pitt, at the site of present-day Pittsburgh.

One by one, the Indian forces captured the string of forts that protected settlers along the western frontier. Each Indian victory left another settlement stranded. In less than two months, the tribes under Pontiac captured

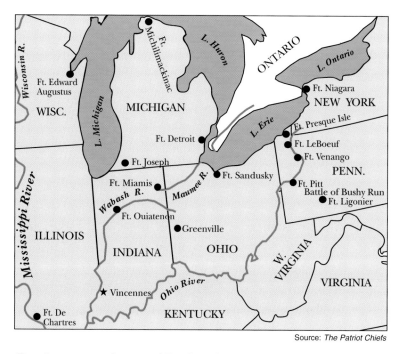

Source: *The Patriot Chiefs*

Pontiac captured most of England's forts along the Great Lakes.

all but three of the British forts in the Great Lakes region. More than two centuries later, Pontiac's brilliant military strategies are studied by students at the U.S. Military Academy at West Point.[6]

The settlers along the frontier, panic-stricken by the Indian successes, formed vigilante groups to fight off attacks. On December 14, 1763, a group of hoodlums known as the Paxton Boys went on a rampage, attacking a peaceful settlement of twenty Christian Indians living in Conestoga, Pennsylvania. They murdered six Indians. Not content with that feat, they followed the survivors to Lancaster, where Pennsylvania officials had taken them for protection. The gang broke down the doors of the workhouse that sheltered the Indian families and viciously killed them all. John Penn, who witnessed the slayings, described the brutality:

> When the poor wretches saw they had no protection . . . they divided into their little families, the children clinging to the parents; they fell on their knees, protested their innocence, declared their love to the English, and that, in their whole lives, they had never done them injury; and in this posture they all received the hatchet! Men, women, and little children were every one inhumanely murdered!—in cold blood![7]

Such acts of viciousness weren't limited to gangs. In the spring of 1764, Commander Amherst called a conference to discuss peace with the Delaware and Shawnee warriors outside Fort Pitt. At the conference, the British gave the Indians blankets that historians believe had been purposely infected with smallpox. Amherst had proposed the tactic in a letter to one of his officers.[8] The deadly disease infected Indian villages all along the frontier.

The nature of Indian society also played a role in the eventual defeat of Pontiac's forces. For centuries, tribes had lived as individual entities, independent of other Indian nations. Pontiac's ability to unite the tribes showed what a great leader he was. But even Pontiac couldn't keep the tribes together for long. After the first victories, several Indians returned to their villages to harvest crops and do other necessary chores. Others, frustrated by the long siege at Fort Detroit, deserted the Ottawa chief.

At the Battle of Bushy Run on August 5, 1763, the English pushed back the tribes and broke the siege at Fort Pitt. Amherst sent fresh troops to shore up the defenses at Fort Detroit and ordered others to retake the forts already captured. At Detroit, Pontiac waited for French forces to come to his aid. The French, however, decided not to do anything that would start another war with England.

With his forces dwindling and no hope of help from the French, Pontiac ended his siege in October and agreed to a truce. The once-mighty chief slipped away to Illinois with a handful of followers. At the Peace Conference at Niagara the next summer, Sir William Johnson, British superintendent of the Indian Territory, signed a peace treaty with most of the northern tribes.

Pontiac, who had been hiding in French villages in Illinois Territory, knew his people could resist no longer. On October 9, 1765, he signed a peace treaty that officially ended Pontiac's Rebellion. By signing the treaty, he lost the last of his followers, who rejected him for giving in to the British. In April 1769, at the age of forty-six, Pontiac was killed by a Peoria Indian.

Shortly after the outbreak of Pontiac's Rebellion, England's King Henry III had issued the Proclamation of October 7, 1763. The proclamation set aside lands west of the Appalachian Mountains as Indian Territory and banned private land sales with Indians.

By the end of the Indian war, however, the American settlers were openly resentful of the interference of officials in faraway England. Many ignored the order, and the steady flow of settlers into Indian land continued.

*A Mohawk chief confers with Sir William Johnson. Members of
the Iroquois tribe signed a treaty with Johnson to set a new
boundary between settlers and the tribes in New York.*

THREE

FRONTIER TREATIES

On a brisk autumn day in October 1768, two thousand members of the Iroquois nation, Shawnees, Mingos, Delawares, and their allies gathered at Fort Stanwix in Rome, New York, to meet with colonial officials. Sir William Johnson, England's superintendent of Indians, and British land agent George Croghan had called the conference to set a new border between colonists and the Indian tribes. Land speculators wanted to open the rich lands west of the Appalachians to English settlers. At their urging, the British Crown had abandoned the Proclamation of 1763 and its promise of an Indian reserve.

It was a day of pageantry. The chiefs wore their finest outfits. The Englishmen came loaded with gifts, hunting supplies, and goods manufactured in England, worth more than ten thousand pounds. They also brought a special cache of gifts, which they secretly gave to the chiefs in exchange for their consent to the land sale.

Enticed by the mound of presents and told the new

boundary would stop settlers from trespassing on the rest of their property, the tribal leaders agreed to sell 1.8 million acres of land to the English negotiators. On November 5, 1768, they signed the Treaty at Fort Stanwix, which gave the British Crown a vast tract of land running from the Mohawk River in central New York to the mouth of the Tennessee River in Kentucky. Only after the sale did the Mohawks (one of the Iroquois tribes) realize their lands lay to the east of the boundary line. In April 1773, they were forced to move onto land occupied by the Oneidas, another Iroquois tribe. "Our lands," they told the neighboring tribe in a plea for refuge, "are all claimed by the white people, even the village where we reside; the very ground under our feet."[1]

William Johnson, who was married to the sister of the powerful Mohawk chief Joseph Brant, helped persuade the Indians to accept the new boundary. Johnson made a substantial profit from the deal. Called the New Purchase by the British, the sale opened to settlers extensive territory in New York, Pennsylvania, West Virginia, and Kentucky. The Penn family, which gained a parcel of land in the deal, got offers from 2,790 eager buyers on the same day they put their land, divided into three-hundred-acre tracts, on the market.[2]

A NEW NATION

During the American Revolution, fought in 1775–1783, most Indian tribes of the East sided with England. The Indians had long traded with the British, who could offer better goods than the rustic Americans. The British also offered protection to the Indians in well-established forts along the battlefront. The Indians knew, too, from long experience that the colonists wanted their land and would do whatever they could to take it from them.

When the war ended in 1783 in the Americans' favor, the tribes faced acts of retribution from their former enemies and received little help from their British allies. During peace negotiations in France, English diplomats surrendered their country's claim to all lands east of the Mississippi River. The Treaty of Paris, which ended the war, completely ignored Indian claims to the lands being bartered by the two nations.

The Indians were outraged. British supporters insisted that the terms should have included the boundaries set by the Fort Stanwix treaty, establishing Indian rights to the lands west of the Ohio River. England wanted the Indian Territory to serve as a buffer between the United States and British-owned Canada. But the American negotiators remained firm. John Jay, chief negotiator for the new United States, noted that his country would not honor any of the treaties made with the Indians by England. "With respect to the Indians," Jay announced, "we claim the right of preemption; with respect to all other nations, we claim the sovereignty over the territory."[3]

Though Jay and other American officials thought the United States should lay claim to all Indian lands, those with more moderate views prevailed. Congress, in one of its first major acts regarding the Indian population, set up the Northwest Territory, a stretch of land covering nearly 170 million acres of prime farmland east of the Mississippi River in what is today the Midwest. The Ordinance of

The new Congress of the United States set aside the Northwest Territory for Indian tribes in what is now the Midwest, but settlers soon claimed much of the land as their own.

1787 put the U.S. government in charge of the new territory, where many of the eastern tribes were now concentrated. But it also promised to respect the tribes' right to their lands:

> The utmost good faith shall always be observed towards the Indians; their lands and their property shall never be taken from them without their consent; and in their

property, rights and liberty, they shall never
be invaded or disturbed, unless in just and
lawful wars authorized by Congress.[4]

While the ordinance recognized the Indians' right to tribal land, land-hungry settlers were already devising treaties to persuade the tribes to part with their property. The new nation forged its first land treaty with the Indians at Fort Stanwix on October 22, 1784. Fitting the mold of previous agreements between the Indians and the English, the pact gave vast lands to settlers in return for token payment to the tribes. The second Fort Stanwix treaty required the Indians to cede all lands in western New York and northwest of the Ohio River. Under that treaty and a second one, made in 1788 between New York State and the Iroquois, the Indians ceded a total of eight million acres.

That was the beginning of a land frenzy that soon consumed Ohio, Kentucky, the remainder of Pennsylvania, and parts of Indiana and New York. As reward for service in the Revolutionary War, Congress gave soldiers more than two hundred thousand acres of land in the Ohio region. Most sold their parcels to land speculators. Congress also granted huge tracts of Ohio territory to several land companies.

In a series of treaties, Indians occupying lands along the Great Lakes and the Ohio Valley ceded millions of acres to the U.S. government. Few of these deals were negotiated in "good faith" or concluded with the consent of the tribe, as stipulated in the Ordinance of 1787. American officials bribed or bullied chiefs into signing treaties

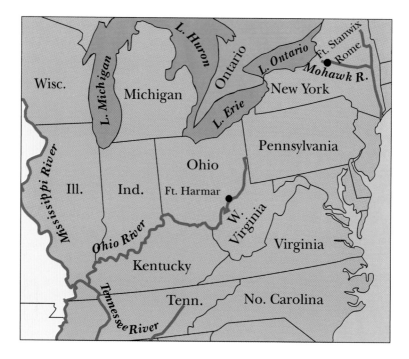

In a series of treaties, tribes ceded much of their lands in western New York, in Ohio, and along Lake Erie.

they didn't understand. The Americans encouraged Indians to drink the rum and whiskey they brought to negotiations, making it easier to cheat the tribes of their land.

The Treaty of Fort McIntosh promised to protect Indians in Ohio from squatters. The Huron, Chippewa, Ottawa, and Delaware chiefs who signed the treaty on January 21, 1785, traded most of their Ohio property for a small tract of protected land, where their tribes would be confined. A "heap of goods" was given to the tribes as a reward for signing the treaty.[5]

On January 9, 1789, the Senecas signed the Treaty of

Fort Harmar, which ceded 202,178 acres of land along Lake Erie. The tribe received about $6,000, or 3¢ an acre, for their property, which was later sold by Congress to Pennsylvania for $151,640.[6] By 1810, Indians owned no land in Pennsylvania.[7]

Historian Henry Adams aptly described the American encroachment on Indian territory, as it ate into the fabric of Indian life:

> No acid ever worked more mechanically on a vegetable fibre than the white man acted on the Indian. As the line of American settlements approached, the nearest Indian tribes withered away.[8]

INDIANS AND SETTLERS CLASH

All along the frontier, settlers and Indians clashed as treaties claimed more traditional hunting grounds and pioneer families moved into the area. During the summer of 1788, Indian warriors began raiding settlements on the fringes of their land. Led by Miami chief Little Turtle and Shawnee chief Blue Jacket, the Indians burned farms and killed families in their attempt to rid the area of settlers. Joining the Miamis and the Shawnees were warriors from the Delaware, Ottawa, Potawatomi, Huron, Chippewa, Kickapoo, Wea, Piankashaw, and Kaskaskia tribes.

By the next autumn, frontiersmen were pushing for all-out war on the Ohio tribes. An expedition of 1,450 men under Brigadier General Josiah Harmar made its way into Indian territory in October 1790, but well-prepared Indian warriors ambushed the army and killed 183 men.

General Arthur St. Clair, governor of the new Northwest Territory, took over the task of quelling the Indian threat. Over the summer of 1791, he raised an army of twenty-three hundred men, some from the militias of the surrounding territories. The U.S. forces followed the Wabash River, reaching the heart of the Indian rebellion in November. By now, St. Clair had problems of his own. Many of his soldiers had deserted or gone home when their enlistments were up, reducing the army to fourteen hundred men. Sick and disabled with gout, the general often had to be carried to the front on a stretcher. St. Clair, who had little experience as a military leader, rejected advice from his officers to send men to scout the area.

Meanwhile, Tecumseh, a young Shawnee warrior, and other Indian scouts kept a close watch on the Americans. They reported that the army had camped along a stream, in an area surrounded by a swamp. Early on the morning of November 3, 1791, one thousand Indian warriors, wielding hatchets and knives, jumped the sleeping soldiers. It turned out to be the U.S. army's worst defeat against Indians in history. At the end of three hours of fierce combat, the Indian force had killed 630 soldiers and wounded another 283. Only 21 Indians lost their lives in the conflict, and 40 were wounded. St. Clair and the surviving soldiers fled to Fort Washington in Ohio.

Terrified by the Indians' victories, hundreds of settlers abandoned their frontier towns for the safety of villages farther east. The Indians, determined to drive all the settlers from the region, continued sporadic attacks on those who remained.

The deepening hostilities between the Indians and the Americans caught the attention of the English. There were many in Canada and England who still wanted to establish an Indian Territory as a buffer between English and American lands. The Paris Peace Treaty had required the English to abandon their forts along the American side of the Great Lakes. Now they restocked Fort Miami, on the Maumee River in the Northwest Territory, and offered the Indians protection from their mutual foe, the Americans. The action convinced the tribes that the British would support them in their fight against the settlers.

While Americans living along the frontier clamored for a war against the Indians, Eastern residents were tired of battle and opposed any further conflicts. Some sympathized with the displaced tribes. Mindful of the public's views, American officials used Iroquois go-betweens to try to negotiate peace with the hostile tribes. They offered to give the Indians $50,000 in goods and make yearly payments of $10,000 in exchange for areas in the Northwest Territory already settled or sold to land companies. The rest of the land north of the Ohio River would remain in Indian hands. But the Indians, confident of the backing of England, rejected the offer. Instead, they demanded that American settlers leave all the lands north of the Ohio River.

That set the stage for war. In the autumn of 1793, General "Mad" Anthony Wayne led a new army of three

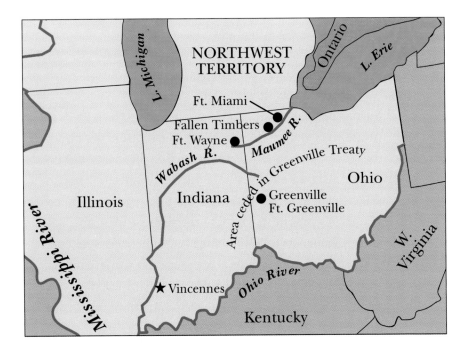

After retreating from General Wayne's forces, Indian tribes ceded huge tracts of land in Ohio and Indiana in the Greenville Treaty.

thousand recruits to Greenville in western Ohio, where they built a fort. A veteran of the Revolutionary War, Wayne was a skilled military leader. Throughout the winter and spring, he drilled his army, preparing them for the battle ahead.

Finally in mid-August, Wayne marched his army to a spot known as Fallen Timbers, along the Maumee River. On the morning of August 20, 1794, the army massed in the clearing. Indian bands soon attacked, but Wayne's well-trained troops forced them to retreat. In less than two hours, the Americans had routed the Indians, who fled in desperation to Fort Miami. When the warriors got to the fort, the British refused to open the gates. With yet another European war threatening, England didn't want to risk a new conflict with the Americans.

The Indians retreated to lands farther west, but they knew without the help of England they could not conquer the Americans. On August 3, 1795, chiefs from the defeated tribes met at Fort Greenville and signed the Greenville Treaty ceding fifteen thousand square miles to the United States. The area included almost two-thirds of Ohio and southeastern Indiana. The tribes were also required to give the Americans sixteen plots for trading posts and allow them to travel on roads and rivers through Indian lands. In return, the Indians received manufactured goods worth $20,000 and a promise of $9,500 worth of goods to be delivered to the tribes and divided among them yearly.

Within just a few years, this treaty, too, had been broken as hundreds of settlers moved into the areas ceded by the tribes and followed the roads and rivers into the lands owned by the Indians.

Tecumseh and William Henry Harrison almost came to blows
during a conference at the Indiana capital of Vincennes.

T<small>ECUMSEH'S</small> R<small>EVENGE</small>

By 1805, most of the grounds where eastern Indians had hunted for generations had been almost completely depleted of game. Unable to feed their families, tribes were forced to sell their remaining lands for annuities paid by the United States government. Much of Indian life had revolved around hunting, especially for the young warriors. The sale of their tribal hunting grounds left the displaced warriors with little to do. Many spent their days drinking the alcohol sold to them by traders.

In an 1801 letter, William Henry Harrison, governor of the Indiana Territory, wrote about the effects of American settlements on Indian culture:

> I can tell at once upon looking at an Indian whom I may chance to meet, whether he belongs to a neighboring or to a more distant tribe. The latter is generally well-

45

clothed, healthy, and vigorous; the former
half-naked, filthy, and enfeebled by intoxi-
cation, and many of them without arms ex-
cepting a knife, which they carry for the
most villainous purposes.[1]

President Thomas Jefferson's solution to the situation
was to encourage Indians to become farmers. But many
of the tribes had hunted for food for centuries. The ro-
bust young warriors, who had proved their manhood by
capturing large game for their tribe, had no interest in
walking behind a plow. Even those tribes that harvested
crops were being forced from their lands by Americans
who wanted to settle there themselves.

With the United States's purchase of the Louisiana
Territory from France in 1803, Jefferson proposed that
eastern tribes be offered land west of the Mississippi to
make room for the settlers in the Ohio, Indiana, and Illinois territories. He viewed the trade as voluntary, reflect-
ing the views he had expressed in a 1786 letter:

It may be regarded as certain that not a
foot of land will ever be taken from the Indians without their own consent. The sa-
credness of their rights is felt by all think-
ing persons in America as much as in Europe.[2]

Despite his lofty views on the Indians' claim to the
land, Jefferson suggested that government trading posts
encourage Indians to go into debt. That way, he noted,

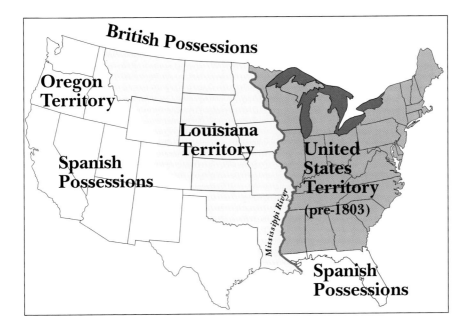

Thomas Jefferson wanted to persuade Eastern tribes to move west of the Mississippi River on lands the United States got from France in the Louisiana Purchase.

the government could further entice Indians to move west in exchange for paying off their debts.[3]

The Indians, however, had no wish to move from their ancestors' lands. And the settlers were not willing to wait until the Indians decided to move on their own. Those pushing their way into the Ohio valley had a friend in William Henry Harrison, governor of the Indiana Territory.

HARRISON AND THE INDIANS

In 1802, Harrison called the Kickapoo, Wea, and Delaware tribes to Vincennes, the capital of the Indiana Territory, to discuss a dispute over the Greenville Treaty.

The resulting agreement, the Treaty of Vincennes, gave additional land to the United States. Harrison claimed his government already owned the disputed land and used bribes and threats to force the tribal leaders to sign the new treaty.

After that, Harrison called conferences every year. With each new treaty, the Indians lost more land. In 1803, the Kaskaskia tribe agreed to cede their lands in Illinois in exchange for Harrison's help in fending off the enemy Potawatomi tribe.

The following year Harrison gave four Sauk and Fox chiefs $2,234.50 in goods and promised yearly payments of $600 to the Sauks and $400 to the Fox tribe in exchange for fifty million acres south of the Wisconsin River and stretching across Wisconsin, Missouri, and Illinois. The land in Missouri had been part of the Louisiana Purchase, which Jefferson had proposed giving to the tribes.

Harrison also agreed to release a tribe member who had been charged with killing an American. Under terms of the treaty, signed in St. Louis on November 3, 1804, the tribes sold the land but were allowed to use it until the federal government claimed it. When the government demanded the land twenty-five years later, a faction of the tribe refused to move. That action sparked the Black Hawk War.

The warrior Black Hawk, who led the uprising, later wrote about the treaty signing in his autobiography. "What do we know of the manners, the laws, and customs of the white people?" he asked. "They might buy our bodies for dissection, and we would touch the goose quill to confirm it and not know what we were doing."[4]

The pattern repeated itself time after time, as the tribes lost vast tracts of their land. Settlers encroached on Indian lands; sporadic attacks broke out between tribes and settlers. Government officials and land speculators, with an eye to expanding their holdings, proposed a treaty to settle the dispute. The Indians got peace, gifts, and a promise of reserved areas set aside for the tribes in exchange for land for settlers. As a preliminary to the proceedings, the negotiators often gave Indian leaders rum and bribed them with gifts. Drunk and eager for the knives, fishhooks, kettles, and gunpowder offered by the Americans, the chiefs signed away their tribes' lands.

The tribes protested, but many times they had no choice but to retreat to the land set aside for them. Almost as soon as the tribe settled on the reserve area that by treaty was to remain in Indian hands "as long as the grass grows and the water flows," frontiersmen on the fringes of the reserve began to poach its game or stake claims inside its borders. Scattered fighting between the Indians and the Americans would once again break out, and the cycle would begin anew.

Demoralized and angry with their leaders for selling their land, the midwestern tribes turned for help to a powerful Shawnee warrior, Tecumseh, and his brother, Tenskwatawa, also called The Prophet.

Tenskwatawa ("Open Door"), seven years younger than Tecumseh, had been an alcoholic dependent on his brother for support. Blind in one eye and suffering from epilepsy, Tenskwatawa had seen a vision of the Creator in

1805 during a trance. As a result, he had given up alcohol and urged his fellow Indians to do the same. Only by following the traditional Indian way of life and by forsaking alcohol and the goods offered by traders, he preached, could the Indian nations regain their former power.

The disheartened Indians looking for a leader were intrigued by The Prophet's message. He soon gained a following among Indians who believed he was a medicine man with psychic powers.

The Prophet's older brother, Tecumseh, viewed with growing alarm the rapid loss of Indian lands. He watched in dismay as settlers overran the land of his ancestors. He saw Indians in surrounding tribes decimated by disease, alcoholism, and poverty. Individual chiefs grew wealthy accepting bribes in exchange for their people's land.

A CONFEDERACY OF WARRIORS

Tecumseh's goal was to unite all the midwestern tribes into a confederacy of warriors. The confederacy would be jointly governed by representatives from all the tribes. In that way, Tecumseh hoped to prevent individual chiefs from giving in to pressure by government agents to sell tribal lands.

While a teenager, Tecumseh had fought for the British during the American Revolution. A brother had died fighting against the Americans in the Battle of Fallen Timbers. A forceful speaker and charismatic leader, Tecumseh preached a message of unification to the followers of The Prophet. The handsome and passionate

Tecumseh drew people to his cause wherever he went. He urged the midwestern tribes to stop fighting among themselves, to end sales of tribal lands, and to unite against the Americans. In making his case before his fellow Indians, the eloquent leader asked:

> Where today are the Pequots? Where the Narragansetts, the Mohicans, the Pokanokets and many other once powerful tribes of our people? They have vanished before the avarice and oppression of the white man, as snow before a summer sun.[5]

Even with the threat to their lands from the encroaching settlers, several of the tribes resisted Tecumseh's efforts. They were afraid to share power with tribes that had been their traditional enemies. However, in 1806, Harrison unwittingly gave the confederation a boost. Mocking The Prophet's claims to supernatural powers, Harrison told members of the Delaware tribe, "If he is really a prophet, ask him to cause the sun to stand still, the moon to alter its course, the rivers to cease to flow."[6] The Prophet, who had learned from Americans that a total eclipse of the sun would occur on June 16, 1806, predicted that the sun would disappear from the sky on that day. When the midday sky turned black at the predicted time, the Indians were astounded. After that, they heeded The Prophet's words without question.

In April 1808, Tecumseh and The Prophet led their followers from Greenville, Ohio, to a safer site in northwestern Indiana, at the junction of the Wabash River and

Tippecanoe Creek. They named the new town, founded on Kickapoo and Potawatomi land, Prophetstown. The Indians set up a farming village, while Tecumseh recruited more followers to strengthen the Indian confederacy. The Shawnee leader told Harrison that he had instructed his people to live in peace:

> Do not take up the tomahawk, should it be offered by the British or by the Long-knives [Americans]; do not meddle with anything that does not belong to you, but mind your own business, and cultivate the ground, that your women and your children may have enough to live on. I now inform you that it is our intention to live in peace with our father and his children forever.[7]

The Prophet often accompanied his brother on his journeys to other tribes. Holding a flaming stick, he invited young warriors to touch his sacred string of beans to show their willingness to join the cause. Intrigued by the medicine man's mysteries and inspired by Tecumseh's fiery speeches, thousands of warriors enlisted in the confederation.

By the end of 1807, the United States had obtained a huge tract of Indian land in Michigan and controlled southern Indiana and most of Illinois. The northern Indians threatened to kill the chiefs who had signed the Michigan treaty. Aware of the tribes' displeasure, U.S. Secretary of War William Eustis wrote to Harrison on July 15, 1809, instructing him to get the consent of "the chiefs of

Source: *The Patriot Chiefs*

Tecumseh and his followers, based at Prophetstown, tried to protect their lands along the Wabash River and the Great Lakes.

all the nations who had or pretended right to these lands" when buying land in the future.[8]

Unrepentant, Harrison invited minor chiefs from the tribes of the Miamis, Eel Rivers, Delawares, Potawatomis, and Kickapoos to a conference at Fort Wayne, Indiana. On September 30, 1809, he persuaded the chiefs to sign the Treaty of Fort Wayne, ceding three million acres of prime hunting land to the United States. In return, their tribes received $7,000 cash and yearly payments of $1,750.

The land included a hundred-mile strip along the Wabash Valley, the only area left where the tribes could hunt enough game to support their villages. Without the hunting grounds, the northern Indians would be forced to seek game in the land of their enemies, the Chippewas and Sioux.

Enraged by the treaty, Tecumseh and his followers charged that the minor chiefs had no power to sell the land. The Potawatomis, they noted, hadn't even owned the land they sold. Outraged Indians from all over the region joined Tecumseh at Prophetstown and demanded the treaty be annulled. The young leader issued a strongly worded protest to Harrison:

> This land that was sold, and the goods that were given for it, was only done by a few. . . . In future we are prepared to punish those chiefs who may come forward to propose to sell their land. If you continue to purchase of them, it will produce war among the different tribes, and at last I do not know what will be the consequence to the white people.[9]

Heading a coalition of Shawnees, Hurons, Kickapoos, Pottawatomies, Ottawas, and Winnebagoes, Tecumseh now commanded six thousand warriors. In the spring of 1810, Tecumseh and his supporters went to Fort Malden in Canada, where the British had a base on the banks of the Detroit River, to ask for weapons. Though eager to cause trouble for the Americans, the British weren't yet ready to start a new conflict. They cautioned Tecumseh to remain at peace until he could build up his forces.

Worried that the Indians' anger over the treaty would lead to war, Harrison invited the chief to meet with him at Vincennes. Accompanied by hundreds of armed warriors, Tecumseh arrived at the capital on August 12, 1810. Harrison met him with a similar entourage of armed observers.

Using an interpreter, Tecumseh told Harrison the Indian confederacy was ready to take up arms to prevent settlers from entering the lands ceded in the Fort Wayne treaty. No longer would Indians allow the American government to deal separately with tribes in an effort to take over their lands. To do so, the chief told Harrison, would mean ruin for his people:

> You want, by your distinctions of Indian tribes, in allotting to each a particular tract of land, to make them to war with each other. . . . You are continually driving the red people; and at last you will drive them into the great lake, where they cannot either stand or work.[10]

At one point during the conference, Tecumseh became so angry he threatened Harrison with his hatchet. The governor drew his sword, but the two agreed to talk over their differences instead of fighting. Both sides left the meeting ready to go to war.[11]

Relations between the United States and the British had worsened. Fearing that trouble with the Indians might start another war with England, President James Madison decided not to send troops to occupy the land ceded under the Fort Wayne treaty. "At this time more particularly," he wrote Harrison, "it is desirable that peace with all the Indian tribes should be preserved."[12]

The winter remained peaceful. On July 27, 1811, Tecumseh and about 300 warriors returned to Vincennes for a second conference with Harrison. Again, nothing was resolved. Tecumseh pledged to keep the peace as long as Harrison did not try to occupy the ceded land. He told the governor he was headed south to gain the support of the Creeks. While he was gone, he said, he had instructed his people at Prophetstown to keep the peace. Tecumseh asked Harrison not to occupy the ceded land along the Wabash Valley until the Indians could meet with the president and settle the matter. The tribes, he noted, needed the lands to hunt food for the winter.

BATTLE AT PROPHETSTOWN

Harrison saw his opportunity to crush the Indian rebellion and make a name for himself. As soon as Tecumseh headed south, he gathered his forces at Vincennes. At Harrison's request, Secretary of War Eustis ordered five hundred soldiers in the Fourth Regiment of the U.S. Infantry to Ohio. For his part, Harrison mustered 130 dragoon members from Kentucky and Indiana and additional volunteers from surrounding areas.

Ignoring Madison's instructions to keep the peace if possible, Harrison headed north with a force of at least nine hundred. On the way to Prophetstown, the army built Fort Harrison, where the governor formally claimed the ceded land for the United States. At the fort, on October 10, an unknown person wounded a soldier on guard. Harrison considered the wounding an act of aggression and declared war.

The army began its march up the Wabash River on October 25. By November 5, the soldiers had crossed into Indian territory and were eleven miles from Prophetstown and Tippecanoe. Alarmed at the army's activities, The Prophet sent messengers to tell Harrison the Indians wanted peace. Harrison agreed to talk with the Shawnee medicine man. Before the meeting could take place, the army marched within 150 yards of the town, then camped for the night. Before dawn on November 7, 1811, a group of six hundred Indians attacked the sleeping soldiers.

Harrison's troops managed to withstand the onslaught, but several key leaders were killed in the battle. The Indians, angry that they had not been able to defeat the soldiers as The Prophet had predicted, abandoned the town. Harrison's army burned Prophetstown and claimed victory over the Indians. The battle gave Harrison the slogan ("Tippecanoe and Tyler, too") that would later carry him to the presidency. Tyler referred to John Tyler, who ran as vice president with Harrison and later became president.

WAR OF 1812

After persuading only a few Creeks to join his cause, Tecumseh returned to find Prophetstown deserted. He was furious at The Prophet for disobeying his order to keep the peace. Gathering his followers, Tecumseh moved to Fort Malden. When war broke out between England and the United States in June 1812, Tecumseh offered his Indian forces to the British. He was made a brigadier general and placed in charge of an Indian army of fifteen thousand warriors.

A brilliant military leader, Tecumseh helped the British win early successes along the U.S.-Canadian border. He planned to capture Fort Meigs on Lake Erie, then take over forts along the Wabash one by one. With those successes, he expected other tribes to join the battle and fight until the Americans had been pushed out of Indian Territory forever.

The war did not turn out that way. On September 10, 1813, U.S. Commodore Oliver Hazard Perry wiped out the British fleet during a three-hour battle on Lake Erie. Cut off from supplies in the East, British Colonel Henry Procter prepared to retreat from Detroit. Ready to stand his ground, a scornful Tecumseh compared the English officer to "a fat animal, that carries its tail upon its back, but when affrighted, he drops it between his legs and runs off."[13]

Harrison's force of three thousand soon drove the Indians and the British to Ontario. The armies met at the Battle of the Thames. At 2:30 P.M. on October 5, Harrison's forces charged the British troops and Tecumseh's warriors. After only a few minutes of fierce battle, Procter and his men fled. A bullet pierced Tecumseh's chest. As The Prophet watched from a hiding place nearby, Tecumseh died. The once-mighty Indian warrior was forty-five years old.

Tecumseh died in fierce fighting at the Battle of the Thames on October 5, 1813.

Tecumseh's death ended the Indian confederation and the Indian war. Though fighting continued along the St. Lawrence River and in the south, the northern Indians' struggle to keep their land was finished, at least until Sauk leader Black Hawk led his people in an uprising in 1832.

As the War of 1812 neared an end, the British once again abandoned their Indian allies—this time at the negotiation table. Even before the fighting ended, negotiators gathered at Ghent, Belgium, to devise a peace treaty between England and the United States. On August 8, 1814, at 1 P.M., the English representative Lord Goulburn presented England's demands. His side required that Indian Territory be established as a buffer between Canada and the United States. The American delegates rejected the proposal.

On August 14, the British team renewed its demands for Indian Territory to be guaranteed along the borders fixed by the Treaty of Greenville. Again, the Americans said no. By this time, one hundred thousand settlers had moved beyond the boundaries set by the Greenville Treaty to Ohio, Indiana, Illinois, and Michigan. The U.S. negotiators adamantly refused to give back the land to the Indians. Agreeing to such English demands, they said, would be "dishonorable to the United States in demanding from them to abandon territory and a portion of their citizens; to admit a foreign interference in their domestic concerns, and to cease to exercise their natural rights on their own shores and in their own waters."[14]

The delegates postponed further negotiations while they waited to see the results of the war. In September, they learned that the British had burned the U.S. Capitol and driven President Madison and his wife, Dolley, to a hiding place in Virginia. Even with that victory, however, the British public was ready to end the war. England had already spent ten million pounds on the conflict, and taxpayers objected to paying higher property taxes to continue the war.

The War of 1812 grew out of disputes between the

United States and England over England's treatment of American merchant ships and American seamen. The British government insisted that ships pay England duties on their goods. England also boarded American ships to search for deserters from the English navy.

Neither country gained much from the war, which ended with the signing of the Treaty of Ghent on December 24, 1814. In the end, the Treaty of Ghent outlined terms of peace and little more. It did not mention the disputes over English duties or boarding of American ships. Likewise, negotiators failed to settle the conflict over Indian territory. The British delegates sent word to their American counterparts that England would be willing to accept the Indian situation as it had been before the war. American delegate Henry Clay accepted the terms, ending discussion of the matter. Only one section of the treaty mentioned Indians, a vaguely worded pledge to grant them the rights they had had before the war. The pledge was never enforced.

While the War of 1812 cost the Americans and the British lives and money, the Indians were the biggest losers. The treaty ended all hope that they could call on foreign allies for help in the fight against the United States for their tribal lands.

*Forced to leave their homeland, many Sauk and Fox Indians
died at the Battle of Bad Axe as they fled from federal troops.*

FIVE

REMOVAL WEST

Disorganized and dispirited, the tribes watched helplessly as settlers filled the Wabash Valley and the lands along Lake Erie, across Indiana and south to Kentucky and Tennessee. In the spring of 1831, a band of Sauk and Fox Indians returned to their homeland in Rock River, Illinois, to plant their crops. When they arrived, they found settlers occupying the land, which was part of a disputed territory ceded in the treaty of 1804 but not claimed by the federal government until twenty-five years later.

Most of the tribe members had moved from Wisconsin and Illinois across the Mississippi River to Iowa with a Sauk leader named Keokuk. But a faction led by Black Hawk, a Sauk warrior, refused to move, claiming that the treaty was invalid. In the fighting that followed, Black Hawk's band was forced into Iowa by federal troops. Many of the Indian men, women, and children died as they tried to cross the Mississippi River to escape gunfire.

Black Hawk, leader of the Sauk tribe

Black Hawk survived and led his people back to their homeland the following spring. Defeated again, Black Hawk was taken prisoner during a battle on August 3, 1832. His captors sent him to Washington, where he was taken on a tour of Eastern cities "to be gazed at."[1]

The Black Hawk War, as the conflict was known, claimed the lives of seventy Americans and five hundred Indians. It was the last war waged by the Indians against

Source: *The Patriot Chiefs*

Sauk and Fox Indians moved to Iowa after being driven from their homelands in Illinois and Wisconsin.

the Americans in the old Northwest Territory. Following the war, Keokuk, who had been made chief, signed a new treaty at Fort Armstrong in Rock Island that ceded 256,000 acres to the United States. The land sold in the Fort Armstrong Treaty covered acreage along the Iowa River west of the Mississippi.

The United States paid a good price for the property at 75¢ an acre. Much of the money ($50,000) went to creditors of the Indians, though the tribe received

$30,000 when the treaty was signed and a $10,000 annuity for ten years. Keokuk arrived at the treaty signing in fancy clothes and riding an elegant horse. Black Hawk, dressed in an old coat and hat and carrying a cane, stood at the back of the group with his two sons. Not allowed to speak or participate in the proceedings, he "looked an object of pity," a "poor dethroned monarch" without a kingdom to rule.[2]

An eloquent speaker, the sixty-seven-year-old former chief later talked of his failed rebellion in 1834:

> My reason teaches me that land cannot be sold. The Great Spirit gave it to his children to live upon, and cultivate, as far as is necessary for their subsistence; and so long as they occupy and cultivate it, they have the right to the soil. . . . Nothing can be sold, but such things as can be carried away.[3]

The Indians were given a month to move from their lands, but most had already taken their belongings to a four-hundred-square-mile area in Iowa reserved for the tribe. Even before the signing, about four hundred settlers had staked claims to the land ceded in the treaty. Within a few years, almost all the northern lands east of the Mississippi had been settled by Americans.

DEFEAT OF THE RED STICKS

Meanwhile, the Southern tribes were fighting their

The Red Sticks killed men, women, and children during the Fort Mims massacre in 1813.

own battles. During the War of 1812, the Southern tribes of Lower Creeks, Cherokees, and Choctaws joined forces with the Tennessee militia led by Andrew Jackson. A faction of Upper Creeks, called Red Sticks, pledged their support to the British. On August 30, 1813, eight hundred Red Sticks attacked Fort Mims, an outpost on the Alabama River approximately thirty-five miles north of Mobile. Wielding their scalping knives, the Red Sticks killed more than three hundred and fifty people seeking refuge at the fort, including settlers' families and pro-American Indians. The blacks at Fort Mims were captured and forced to serve as the Red Sticks' slaves.

In retaliation for the Fort Mims massacre, Jackson's forces killed seven hundred Red Sticks and their allies at the Battle of Horseshoe Bend on March 27, 1814. The Red Sticks who survived fled to Florida and joined forces with the Seminole tribe there.

In July 1814, Jackson rounded up the friendly Creek chiefs who had helped him defeat the Red Sticks. He told them they would have to cede two-thirds of their land to the United States. Initially, the chiefs refused, but Jackson told them if they tried to join their rebel brothers, the militia would wipe them out before they reached Florida. Left with little choice, the chiefs signed the Treaty of Fort Jackson on August 9, 1814. In the treaty, the Creeks agreed to part with their lands in the southern and western regions of Alabama. They also agreed to allow military posts and roads to be built on their remaining tract of land.

Southern planters, eager for fertile farmland, soon took over the ceded Creek territory. They complained that their runaway slaves were escaping into Florida. Spain claimed possession of Florida, but most of the lands were occupied by Seminole Indians and other tribes.

Posses from Georgia began attacking Indian villages along the Florida border, in search of runaway slaves. Bands of Seminoles retaliated with raids of their own.

Red Stick warriors massacred Americans seeking shelter at Fort Mims. Andrew Jackson retaliated by killing hundreds of Red Sticks at the Battle of Horseshoe Bend.

When the Seminoles attacked a boat carrying soldiers and their families, Jackson used the incident as an excuse to invade Florida. Jackson's army, again aided by Creek allies, swept through the southeastern territory, burning Seminole villages and quickly quelling the rebellion, later called the First Seminole War. Spain, weakened by raging wars in Europe, wanted to avoid a conflict in America. It agreed to sell its Florida property to the United States.

The Adams-Onís Treaty, signed by Spain and the United States on February 22, 1819, made no mention of the tribes occupying the region.

AMERICAN DESTINY

In the fifty years since the colonists had set up an independent nation on the North American continent, the population of the United States had skyrocketed. Settlers had pushed across the Appalachian ridge and now poured into the fertile valleys between the mountains and the Mississippi River. In the eyes of many Americans, it was their right—their destiny—to claim those lands. William Henry Harrison, governor of the Indiana Territory and later president, championed those views:

> Is one of the fairest portions of the globe
> to remain in a state of nature, the haunt of
> a few wretched savages, when it seems des-
> tined by the Creator to give support to a
> large population and to be the seat of civi-
> lization?[4]

One of those "wretched savages," Choctaw chief Shulush Homa, had his own views on the subject, which he expressed in a December 1824 letter to Secretary of War John C. Calhoun:

> It has been a great many years since our
> white brothers came across the big waters
> and a great many of them has not got civi-

lized yet; therefore we wish to be indulged in our savage state of life until we can have the same time to get civilized . . . [and] for that reason we think we might as well enjoy our right as well as our white brothers.[5]

Americans and Indians held differing views on what was "civilized." To Americans, being civilized meant adopting their way of life. Missionaries converted scores of Indians to Christianity. The Cherokee, Chickasaw, Creek, Choctaw, and Seminole tribes became known as the "Five Civilized Tribes" because they adopted much of American culture.

Adopting American society's ways, however, did not protect the tribes from land fever. The Southerners wanted the Indians' land. They were determined to get it regardless of how "American" the tribes became.

Andrew Jackson, who had won the presidency in 1828, had little sympathy for the Indians. In 1817 he had rejected the idea of Indian rights in a letter to James Monroe:

I have long viewed treaties with the Indians an absurdity not to be reconciled to the principles of our government. . . . The Indians are the subjects of the United States, inhabiting its territory and acknowledging its sovereignty.[6]

In the past, Congress had supported, on paper at least, the right of Indians to their land. This policy was es-

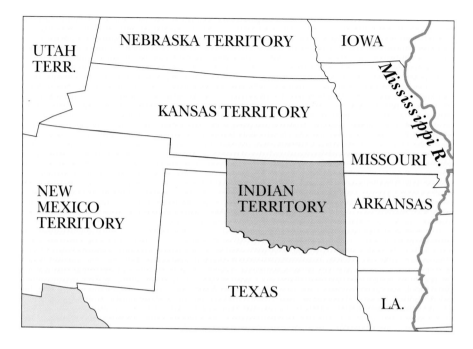

Land west of the Mississippi was set aside as Indian Territory. The area would later become the state of Oklahoma.

tablished by the Ordinance of 1787 when it set up Indian Territory west of the Appalachians.

Jackson planned to change that. He proposed that Indians be moved from their lands in the east and offered an equal amount of land to the west of the Mississippi in what was known as the "Great American Desert." No Americans, presumably, would ever want to settle there. The area was dubbed Indian Territory, a vast expanse that would later include the state of Oklahoma. If the Indians did not move voluntarily, Jackson said, the government would force them to go west.

Some supporters of the Indians argued that the move

would benefit the tribes by rescuing them from the influence of alcohol and other evils introduced by Americans.
Others contended that the move would provide the Indians with a fair deal, while ending the conflict between settlers and the tribes.

Several Congressmen argued vehemently against the
bill. Senator Theodore Frelinghuysen of New Jersey asked
in disgust, "Is it one of the prerogatives of the white man,
that he may disregard the dictates of moral principles,
where an Indian shall be concerned?"[7]

After a bitter debate, Congress passed the Indian Removal Act on May 28, 1830. The Act required tribes east
of the Mississippi River to move to western lands. Tribes
would be given the chance to negotiate treaties outlining
details of the move. Each tribe would be allotted property in the west equal to their tribal lands.

The states began taking similar measures. In 1829, Alabama annexed all Indian land in that state. In March
1830, the Mississippi legislature enacted a law prohibiting
tribes from practicing ancient rituals. Under the law,
chiefs who led their people in such rituals would be fined
and jailed. That same year, the Mississippians ordered
Choctaws and Chickasaws out of the state and voted to
abolish "all rights, privileges, immunities, and franchises
held, claimed, or enjoyed by those persons called Indians
within the chartered limits of the State."[8]

Left with little recourse, the Choctaws, on October 28,
1830, signed the Treaty of Dancing Rabbit Creek, in
which the tribe agreed to move west. The treaty granted
the tribe 140,000 acres west of the Mississippi, but
crooked land deals enabled land speculators to get more

than half of the land. As a reward for signing the treaty, two half-white leaders of the tribe received large tracts of land along the Tennessee River. Almost four thousand members of the tribe died on the trip west, freezing to death in the Oklahoma snow or starving along the trail. One observer later called the Indians' forced move "next to a system of deliberate murder."[9]

CORRUPTION AND FRAUD

The Chickasaws, who at first rejected the treaty, agreed to the move after being promised they could approve the western plot where they would settle. During the delay, speculators took over businesses and property on the tribe's eastern territory and cheated tribe members out of payment for their land.

The Creeks suffered a similar fate. Coerced into signing a treaty on March 24, 1832, the tribe suffered greatly at the hands of dishonest land speculators and uncaring federal agents before their move west. Land speculators paid Indians $5 to $10 to pose as land owners and sign fraudulent deeds.[10] Greedy officials appointed to represent Creeks who died during the wait cheated heirs out of their inheritances. A later report verified that in some towns nineteen out of twenty Creek land deals were the work of crooks, both American and Indian.[11]

Article Twelve of the Creek treaty had stipulated that "this . . . shall not be construed so as to compel any Creek Indian to emigrate, but they shall be free to go or stay, as they please."[12] The Creeks, once renowned craftsmen who had lived in well-built cabins and farms along the

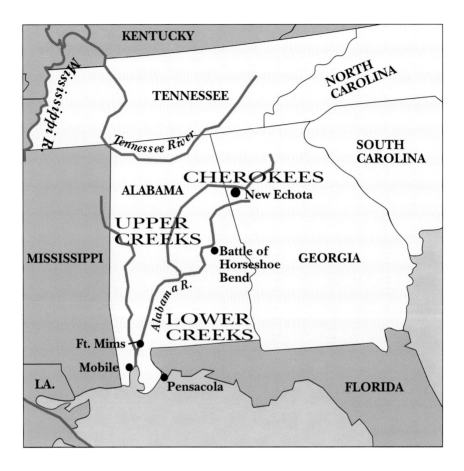

The Creek and Cherokee tribes had extensive land holdings in Georgia, Tennessee, Alabama, North Carolina, and South Carolina.

Mississippi Delta, were now without food, land, or money. They had no recourse but to move west.

Robert L. Crawford, a U.S. marshal who observed the treatment of the Creeks with disgust, said of the March 1832 treaty:

I have never seen corruption carried on to such proportions in all my life. A number of the land purchasers think it rather an honor than a dishonor to defraud the Indian out of his land.[13]

In the winter of 1836–1837, almost fifteen thousand Creeks began the thousand-mile trek west. The defeated figures made their way through the Oklahoma snow, some walking with bare feet across the icy ground. All along the trail, belongings littered the way where the travelers had been forced to drop them. Government troops accompanying the sad caravan promised that the abandoned treasures would be delivered later, but the promise was never kept. Vultures flying overhead marked where the dead Indians lay.

'Spare Our People!'

The Cherokees had a word for Americans: *econnaunuxulgee,* which meant "people-greedily-grasping-after-land." Of the five tribes, the Cherokees had become most like the American society that surrounded them. They had their own written language, paid taxes, and ran eighteen schools. In 1827, the tribe had adopted a constitution based on that of the United States and had established its own court system and two-house legislature with elected officials. Indians of the tribe read their own newspaper, printed in both English and Cherokee.

According to the 1825 census, fifteen thousand Cherokee Indians lived on tribal lands in central Georgia, Tennessee, Alabama, North Carolina, and South Carolina. The richest of the five tribes, the Cherokees ran plantations and owned thirteen hundred slaves. The 1825 census figures show the tribe had twenty-two thousand head of cattle, seven hundred looms, two thousand spinning wheels, and hundreds of plows.[14] Grist mills, cotton gins, and saw mills manufactured goods for the tribe to use and to sell.

Though some Cherokees still practiced ancient Indian customs, most of the tribe lived much like their American neighbors. Many had married American settlers; as a result a large number of Cherokees had English names.

In 1802, Georgia had agreed to turn over its claims to western lands to the federal government in exchange for a promise that the United States would give up its control of land occupied by the Cherokee tribe. Georgia officials claimed title to all Cherokee land in Georgia in 1828, based on the fact that their forebears had "discovered" the land.

In July 1829, gold was found on Cherokee land. That made the Georgians even more eager to claim rights to the territory. More than two thousand gold seekers flooded the area. State and federal officials did nothing to stop them from trespassing on Indian property. On December 19, 1829, Georgia legislators passed laws disbanding the Indian government and banning Cherokees from mining the gold on their land. The only official function the Cherokees were allowed to perform was to sign treaties. Meeting in secret at their capital in New Echota, Georgia, the Cherokee National Council voted that anyone who sold tribal lands would be executed.

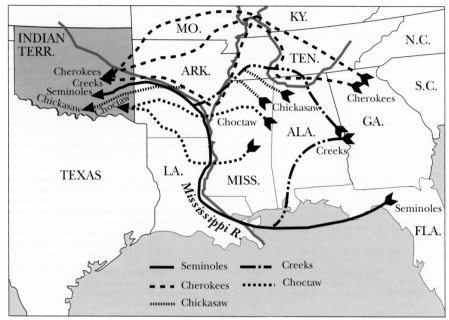

Source: *The American Heritage Book of Indians* and *Compton's Encyclopedia*

Members of the Five Civilized Tribes were forced to leave their lands in the South and resettle in Indian Territory.

The tribe's sophisticated leaders carried their battle with Georgia to the U.S. Supreme Court. The Court refused to interfere in Georgia's claim to Cherokee land. But Supreme Court Chief Justice John Marshall ruled in the 1831 case that the federal government was responsible for protecting the tribes, which he described as "domestic dependent nations."[15]

Undeterred, the Cherokees once again turned to the courts for help. In another landmark case, *Worcester v. Georgia,* Justice Marshall ruled in 1832 that the Cherokee nation was a "distinct community, occupying its own territory, with boundaries accurately described, in which the laws of Georgia can have no force, and which the citizens of Georgia have no right to enter, but with the consent of the Cherokees themselves, or in conformity with treaties, and with the Acts of Congress."[16] He added, "A weaker power does not surrender its independence—its right to self-government—by association with a stronger and [by] taking its protection."[17]

The Cherokees rejoiced when they heard Marshall's words. Now, they assumed, the tribe would be allowed to stay on its ancestral land. But President Andrew Jackson was determined to move the Indians out of the east. When he learned of the court ruling, he is said to have replied, "John Marshall has rendered his decision, now let him enforce it."[18]

Assured that Jackson would not interfere, the Georgians set up a lottery in 1833 to dole out the Cherokee land in their state. Many of the Cherokee leaders were forced to give up their plantations. When lottery winners claimed the tribe's government buildings, the Cherokees set up a new capital in Tennessee.

A faction of the tribe, led by Major Ridge, his son John, and his nephew Elias Boudinot, believed the situation was hopeless. The Indian leaders feared the entire Cherokee nation would be destroyed if the tribe did not give up its lands and move west. On December 29, 1835, they signed the Treaty of New Echota with the U.S. government. Boudinot and Major Ridge were later executed by members of the tribe for signing the treaty.

Under the treaty's terms, the leaders ceded 4,509,280

acres of Cherokee land in Georgia, 1,611,520 acres in Alabama, 949,760 acres in Tennessee, and 711,680 acres in North Carolina. In exchange, the tribe received seven million acres of land in Indian Territory and $5 million, which the government retained for the tribe's use.

After the leaders signed the treaty, Jackson ordered his agent, John F. Schermerhorn, to arrange a conference with the tribe. Of the more than sixteen thousand tribe members, only seventy-nine attended the conference.[19] Schermerhorn, claiming that all those not at the meeting favored the treaty, used the fraudulent report to prove the tribe's support for the terms.

The federal agent sent to record tribe members in preparation for the move west contradicted Schermerhorn's claims. In an April 12, 1936, letter to Secretary of War Lewis Cass, Major William M. Davis wrote:

> That paper called a treaty is no treaty at all because not sanctioned by the great body of Cherokees, and made without their participation or assent. I solemnly declare to you that upon its reference to the Cherokee people it would be instantly rejected by nine-tenths of them and I believe by nineteen-twentieths of them. . . . I now warn you and the President that if the paper of Schermerhorn called a treaty is sent to the Senate and ratified you will bring trouble on the Government and eventually destroy this Nation [the Cherokees]. The Cherokees are a peaceable, harmless peo-

ple, but you may drive them to desperation, and this treaty cannot be carried into effect by the strong arm of force.[20]

Vehement in their opposition to the treaty, the members of the largest Cherokee faction embarked on a tireless lobbying campaign in Washington, D.C. Their leader, John Ross, a Cherokee tribe member, journeyed to the U.S. capital time after time, talking to members of Congress and the Senate. Several influential people supported the tribe's cause, among them Senator Henry Clay; Colonel David Crockett, who had fought with Jackson against the Red Stick Indians during the War of 1812; Senator Daniel Webster, and U.S. Representative Edward Everett. In one last desperate act, the tribe delivered a powerful plea to the House and Senate in 1836. It read in part:

> We are deprived of membership in the human family. We have neither land nor home nor resting place that can be called our own. . . . In truth our cause is your own. It is the cause of liberty and justice. It is based on your own principles which we have learned from yourselves; for we have gloried to count your Washington and Jefferson as our great teachers. . . . Before your august assembly we present ourselves, in the attitude of deprecation and of entreaty. On your kindness, on your humanity, on your compassions, on your benevo-

lence, we rest our hopes. To you we address
our reiterated prayers. Spare our people!
Spare the wreck of our prosperity![21]

The entreaty did no good. The House tabled the
Cherokees' request to stop the enforced move. On May
23, 1836, the Senate ratified the Treaty of New Echota by
one vote. The tribe was given two years to move west; after that, the Indians would be forced from their tribal
lands.

The Cherokees in the Ridge faction soon moved to
Indian Territory, but the rest of the tribe remained in
their eastern homes. As the deadline neared, Georgia of-
ficials threatened to call in the state militia to move the
Cherokees west if the federal government put off its duty.
On the appointed day, May 23, 1838, General Winfield
Scott and seven thousand federal troops marched into
the Cherokee towns to begin the removal.

Bargain hunters crowded the streets of the Cherokee
towns, eager to get a deal on household goods, buildings,
and other property. The Indians, desperate to sell their
possessions before the move, agreed to prices far below
the true value. A Cherokee man told of the auction held
at his house in those last frantic days before the trek west.
His family's china, edged in blue, sold for 25¢ a plate. He
never received the money from the auction, which likely
ended up in the pockets of the auctioneer.[22]

Those who didn't sell their belongings were promised
the goods would be brought to them in their new village.
Instead, thugs broke windows, smashed doors, and looted
the Indians' homes as soon as the army forced the occu-

Four thousand members of the Cherokee tribe died on the thousand-mile trek to Indian Territory in Oklahoma.

pants to leave. Wrote one historian, "Many an Indian turning for a farewell look saw his house going up in flames."[23]

Indians were herded into camps under armed guard to wait for the trip to begin. Almost eighteen thousand Cherokee men, women, and children "were rounded up like cattle," one observer wrote.[24] Soldiers kept the line moving, prodding with their bayonets those who walked slowly. One man whose spouse had been pricked by a bayonet lashed out against the offending soldier. The troops handcuffed him and lashed him one hundred times with a whip.[25] The sick and dying were carried into the camps on stretchers.

Four hundred Indians escaped into the mountains, where they lived until 1842. Their descendants, known as the Eastern Cherokees, remain in the region today, living on a sixty-thousand-acre reservation in North Carolina.

TRAIL OF TEARS

The others began their forced march through one thousand miles of rough terrain and wilderness. Like the Chickasaws, Creeks, and Choctaws before them, the Cherokees suffered immeasurable sadness and pain along the Trail of Tears, as the march came to be known.

Throughout the winter of 1838 to 1839, the Indians walked. Food left for them by government agents rotted on the trail before they reached it. Wolves followed the stragglers, digging up the graves of the dead left behind. As many as one hundred people died in a single day; four thousand died before the walk had ended. After six months of horror—broken-spirited, sick, and starving—the Cherokees straggled into Indian Territory country.

In his December 1838 message to Congress, Martin Van Buren, now president, reported that the Removal Act had "had the happiest effects. . . . The Cherokees have emigrated without any apparent reluctance."[26]

Before the last group of Cherokees left their homeland in the east, the Cherokee National Council issued one last edict:

> The title of the Cherokee people to their lands is the most ancient, pure and absolute known to man; its date is beyond the reach of human record; its validity confirmed by possession and enjoyment antecedent to all pretense of claim by any portion of the human race.
>
> The free consent of the Cherokee people is indispensable to a valid transfer of the Cherokee title. The Cherokee people have neither by themselves nor their representatives given such consent. It follows that the original title and ownership of lands still rests in the Cherokee Nation, unimpaired and absolute. The Cherokee people have existed as a distinct national community for a period extending into antiquity beyond the dates and records and memory of man. These attributes have never been relinquished by the Cherokee people, and

cannot be dissolved by the expulsion of the Nation from its territory by the power of the United States government.[27]

Their words resounded with truth and honor. Then, in defeat, they joined their people in the west.

SECOND SEMINOLE WAR

The Seminoles had been told they could keep their Florida land for twenty years when they signed the Treaty of Camp Moultrie on September 18, 1823. The treaty also guaranteed the tribe an annuity of $5,000 for twenty years.

Less than nine years later, James Gadsden, sent by Jackson, coerced fifteen minor Seminole chiefs into agreeing to move the tribe west. Payne's Landing Treaty, signed May 9, 1832, allowed Seminole delegates to travel west of the Mississippi, approve the land selected for the tribe, and relocate three years later. They would be paid for the property they left behind and get an equal amount of land in the west.

A severe drought had left the Seminoles starving and desperate for food. The tribe resisted the terms of the treaty, but Gadsden promised them food if they consented to the move. He took six Indians to Indian Territory to view the proposed site. Used to Florida's mild climate, the Indians found the chilly air too cold for their tribe. But Jackson, eager to finish the relocation, ordered the move to take place quickly. He also wanted the Seminoles to join the Creeks on one site in the west. The president threatened to pay the Seminoles' annuity to the Creek tribe if they didn't agree to his proposal.

The Seminole delegates were brought to Fort Gibson in Indian Territory on March 28, 1833. Told they could not return to Florida until they signed the document before them, the delegates endorsed a report stating that they approved of the western site and that they agreed to join the Creek tribe. Jackson used the delegates' report to convince the Senate to ratify the Treaty of Payne's Landing.

This new trickery was too much for the tribe. Hiding in the Florida swamps and forests, the Seminoles fiercely fought the federal troops sent to take them west. The most expensive Indian war in U.S. history, the Second Seminole War raged from late in 1835 to 1842. Osceola, a Red Stick Creek who as a teenager had fought Jackson's troops during the First Seminole War, led Seminole warriors in their hide-and-seek raids on American troops. In 1837, American army officers called a truce and asked to meet with Osceola. When he emerged from the wilderness, U.S. troops seized him and held him in chains at Fort Moultrie in Charleston, South Carolina.

The Seminole leader's health soon failed. As Osceola lay dying on his prison bed, his family helped the young warrior don his war costume. With great care, he put on his powder horn, bullet pouch, and war belt. Methodically, he applied the red paint of war to half his face, his wrists, and his hands. Atop his head he wore a headdress decorated with three ostrich feathers. Then, grasping his scalping knife in his right hand, he died.[28]

Osceola's death made the Seminoles more deter-

Indian forces led by Osceola attacked Fort King in Florida in 1835.

mined than ever to evade the army. They fought on for another four years. Florida officials, equally determined to capture the tribe, offered to pay $200 for each Indian captured, dead or alive. The army seized four thousand Seminoles, who were taken under guard to Indian Territory. Another fifty or sixty Indians were killed during the fighting. But a small band of Indians escaped to the Everglades, where their descendants live today. The effort to move the Seminoles west cost the United States an estimated $40 million and the lives of fifteen hundred soldiers.

In all, sixty thousand members of the Seminole, Cherokee, Chickasaw, Creek, and Choctaw tribes were forced from their homes and moved west. Jackson's old Indian allies had effectively been eliminated from the east.

*Homesteaders rushed across the border into Oklahoma to claim
land that Indian tribes had controlled for hundreds of years.*

Six

WESTERN TRIBES

More than 90,000 eastern Indians made the journey across the Mississippi River between 1830 and 1840 as a result of the Indian Removal Act. Most of the tribes allowed to remain in the east were in sparsely populated areas like Maine and along Florida's Gulf coast. With the help of the Quakers, some members of the Iroquois tribes in New York state managed to avoid deportation as well. By the 1840s, most of the eastern tribes were gone.

The commissioner of Indian Affairs, T. Hartley Crawford, issued an 1838 report, referring to the removal as "a change of residence effected under treaties, and with the utmost regard to their [the Indians'] comfort."[1] The report continued, "We will have quietly and gently transported 18,000 friends to the west bank of the Mississippi."[2]

The Indians' forced march was far more than the change of residence Crawford reported. It had shredded the fabric of the Indians' lives. Spouses, children, and parents were dead. Tribes were separated; families split into factions. Their property and wealth were gone.

With little left from their pasts, the survivors of the arduous trip west focused on setting up villages and learning to live in the alien land where they had been driven. But the transition wasn't easy. They had to cope with poverty and a harsh climate. Despondent Indians succumbed to alcoholism, buying whiskey and rum at the shops set up by traders along the Indian borders. Eight hundred Cherokee families who had settled in Arkansas sought the government's protection when drunk tribesmen went on a robbery and killing rampage.[3]

The new arrivals also faced the anger of the Plains Indians, who claimed the western lands as their own. In 1854, one thousand warriors from the Comanche, Kiowa, Osage, and Cheyenne tribes attacked a band of one hundred Sac and Fox Indians as they hunted buffalo on the Kansas plains. The buffalo hunters managed to shoot off the raiders, who had no guns, but not before twenty-six of their number were killed.

'AS LONG AS GRASS GROWS'

Even in this new country, the transplanted tribes were pursued by Americans hungry for land. In 1854, a band of Cherokees signed a treaty granting them land in Kansas Territory "as long as grass grows and water flows."[4] At that time, there weren't a thousand settlers in the region. Beginning in 1859, the tribe was forced to sign several new treaties that ceded portions of their land to settlers pushing into the area. On April 27, 1868, the Kansas Cherokees signed a final treaty that gave away the remainder of their land and forced them to join their tribe members in Indian Territory.

The Civil War dealt another blow to the transplanted southern tribes. Most members of these tribes joined the Confederates' battle against the North. They were promised a say in the Confederate government, invited to send representatives to the rebels' congress, and told they could tax traders on their lands. When the South lost the war, Congress dealt much more harshly with the Indians than with their Confederate allies. While the Southerners were allowed to retain their boundaries and continue to operate as individual states, the Indians who had fought for the Confederacy were stripped of half their land. Congress repealed the tribes' treaties and replaced them with less favorable pacts that forced the Indians out of the western half of Indian Territory into the eastern region.

The tribes that had fought for the North during the war didn't fare much better. U.S. agents cheated many of the fifteen thousand warriors who had sided with the Union out of their pensions and army pay.

GOLD RUSH DOOMS PLAINS INDIANS

The Plains Indian tribes met a similar fate. A series of treaties eventually forced thirty Plains tribes into the least desirable parts of the western region of Indian Territory.

For centuries these tribes—among them the Comanches, Sioux, Cheyenne, and Blackfeet—had relied on buffalo for food and clothing. With the discovery of gold in California in 1849, thousands of adventurers journeyed west, eager to get rich quick in the hills a continent away. Wagon trains bringing gold seekers began traveling through the Indians' traditional hunting grounds.

The tribes attacked the caravans passing through their lands. After the army marched into the area, the Indians agreed to meet at Fort Laramie in Wyoming to work out a deal between the wagon trains and the tribes. Under the Fort Laramie Treaty of 1851, signed in September, the Plains Indians agreed to stay away from certain wagon train routes. The government, in return, promised to keep adventurers and settlers out of Indian Territory.

In 1858 and 1859, a new surge of fortune hunters headed west across Indian lands after gold was discovered at the foot of the Rocky Mountains in Montana. The government tried to force a new treaty, which would have shunted the Indian tribes onto reservations. The Indians refused the new terms. When war threatened in 1861, some bands—well aware of the force of the U.S. Army—tried to seek peace for their followers.

One group of Cheyenne Indians headed for shelter at Fort Lyon in Colorado. President Abraham Lincoln and Colorado Governor John Evans had reassured the group's leader, Black Kettle, that the Indians would be safe at the fort. But Colonel John Chivington, in charge of Colorado volunteers, issued other orders to his men: "The Cheyennes will have to be soundly whipped before they will be quiet. If any of them are caught in your vicinity, kill them, as that is the only way."5

Early on the morning of November 29, 1864, a troop of Colorado volunteers opened fire on the sleeping Indi-

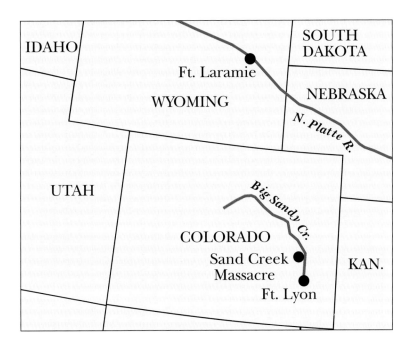

Colorado militiamen massacred two hundred Cheyenne Indians at Sand Creek as their leader, Black Kettle, waved a white flag of truce.

an village, which was camped along Sand Creek forty miles from Fort Lyon. Black Kettle stood in front of his tipi, waving an American flag that President Lincoln had given him and a white flag of truce. The troops ignored these signs of peace, preferring instead to slaughter as many men, women, and children as they could. People in the village ran to the creek and dug holes in the sand to hide.

When the survivors finally dared to return to the village, they found two hundred Indians dead. Many had been mutilated; some cut open with hunting knives, others clubbed with guns.

WESTWARD HO!

Back East, Americans protested the army's treatment of innocent Indians. Horrified at the reports of atrocities like that at Sand Creek, they pushed for a peaceful settlement of the controversy between Indians and settlers. But the goal remained the same: to clear the way for American expansion west. Developers of a railroad that would link the East Coast cities with those on the West Coast wanted to lay track through Indian country. Investors wanted to set up operations in the region's mines. Pressure mounted to open the Plains to settlers looking for farmland.

Those seeking a diplomatic settlement persuaded several minor chiefs to sign treaties to move their tribes onto reservations in the Dakotas. The stronger tribes resisted. Determined to clear a path—known as the Bozeman Trail—to the Montana mines, the army began an all-out campaign to drive the remaining tribes onto reservations.

In June 1866, federal agents called a convention of Sioux tribes at Fort Laramie, presumably to negotiate a peace settlement. The agents' offer of gifts and money for the right to go through Indian land to build the Bozeman Trail appealed to many at the gathering, who had had a poor hunting season. The agents also pledged to keep travelers who passed over the trail off Indian property.

Many Indians seemed ready to agree to the proposal when Colonel Henry Carrington arrived with seven hundred soldiers in tow. The army officer told the gathering that he was on his way to build forts through Indian country to protect the road builders who would construct the Bozeman Trail.

Red Cloud, a war chief of the Sioux tribe of Oglala Lakotas, was furious at the attempt to trick his people. Warning those at the convention not to approve the treaty, he said:

> The white men have crowded the Indians back year by year until we are forced to live in a small country north of the Platte, and now our last hunting ground, the home of the People, is to be taken from us. Our women and children will starve, but for my part I prefer to die fighting rather than by starvation.[6]

A few tribes signed the treaty agreeing not to interfere with the building of the road. For their support, they were promised yearly payments of $70,000 for twenty years.

Most of the tribes, however, supported Red Cloud. Over the next year, the forces under Red Cloud and Sioux leader Sitting Bull attacked travelers along the trail, raided work parties, and surrounded forts built by Carrington's men.

In one fierce battle on December 21, 1866, Sioux warriors lured Captain William Fetterman and the eighty men under his command into an ambush along the Bozeman Trail near Fort Philip Kearny. An estimated two thousand Sioux warriors swooped down on the soldiers,

The Bozeman Trail offered a more direct route to the gold mines of Montana, but a Sioux uprising closed the road.

killing them all. American troops found the dead stripped naked, scalped, and mutilated. Carrington, who commanded the forces at Fort Kearny, described the condition of the bodies:

> Eyes torn out and laid on rocks; noses cut off; ears cut off; chins hewn off; teeth chopped out; joints of fingers, brains taken out and placed on rocks with other members of the body; entrails taken out and exposed; hands cut off; feet cut off; arms taken out from sockets.[7]

Faced with mounting costs, loss of lives, and criticism from peace advocates in the East, the government finally abandoned the Bozeman Trail.

In 1868, Red Cloud rode into Fort Laramie accompanied by 125 leaders of the Sioux tribes to negotiate peace. The treaty signed by the victorious Indian leader formally ended the army's attempt to open the Bozeman Trail. The soldiers abandoned the forts and left the Indian grounds to the tribes.

It was a short-lived victory. Government agents soon set up a reservation in South Dakota where they intended to force the Sioux tribes to live. When Red Cloud and other chiefs objected, they were taken to Washington, D.C., where the secretary of the interior produced a copy of the treaty they had signed. The U.S. officials claimed the treaty had stipulated that the tribes go to the reservation, but the chiefs contended they had never heard of such a requirement when they signed the treaty.

With support from Eastern sympathizers, Red Cloud won concessions from the government. In 1871, the chief and his followers were allowed to live on a tract of land along the North Platte River. But two years later, the government forced the band to move north to another plot reserved for them to make way for the railroad and American settlers.

CUSTER'S LAST FIGHT

According to the treaty of 1868, the western half of South Dakota was set aside as reserved lands for the Sioux. Many Sioux already lived there in the Black Hills, where Indians had traditionally gone to pray and worship. In 1874, Lieutenant Colonel George Custer and his army surveyed the region. Despite the terms of the treaty, which banned non-Indians even from walking through the area without Indian permission, the federal government planned to build a fort in the Black Hills.

While on this duty, Custer discovered gold in the hills. His announcement caused a stampede of gold seekers into the Indians' reserved lands. Outraged, the Indians threatened to kill the invaders.

Seeking to head off war, federal agents met with twenty thousand Sioux in September 1875 at Red Cloud's reservation in South Dakota. Red Cloud proposed to sell the Black Hills for $600 million; the federal agents gave a counteroffer of $6 million.

When the Indians refused to consider the offer, President Grant ordered General George Crook to herd the Indians onto reservations outside the area.

In March, one unit of Crook's army attacked a group of Cheyennes beyond the North Platte River. Oglala war chief Crazy Horse (Tashunke Witko) soon joined the Cheyennes and succeeded in holding off the cavalry until the Cheyennes could escape. Seeking shelter from the wintery cold, Crook led his men back to the North Platte River.

Leading the Indian resistance, Crazy Horse brought one thousand Sioux warriors to a huge Indian village nestled in the valley of the Little Big Horn River. As many as ten thousand Indians from various Sioux tribes lived there. Sitting Bull (Tatanka Iyotake) and other noted war chiefs joined Crazy Horse at Little Big Horn.

Six thousand Indian warriors slaughtered George Custer and the 208 men under his command at the Battle of Little Big Horn.

Meanwhile, two other units of Crook's army had met to the north along the Yellowstone River. They planned to move south, trapping the Indians between their forces and Crook's men. They didn't know the size of the Indian forces and didn't realize that Crook's unit had retreated. An advance party of six hundred troopers from the U.S. Seventh Cavalry, led by George Custer, set out toward the Indian village.

Approaching the village, Custer sent one section of his troops to the south and another to the west to investigate the surrounding area. On June 25, 1876, Custer—underestimating the Indian forces—led the rest of his men on a surprise attack of the encampment. Six thousand warriors, under the command of Crazy Horse, massed quickly around Custer's men. In less than half an hour, Custer and all 208 of his men lay dead. Viewing Custer's dead body, Sitting Bull was reported to have said, "Long Hair [Custer] thought he was the greatest man in the world. Now he lies there."[8]

It would be the Sioux's last major victory against the U.S. Army. Fired up by what headlines called a massacre, Americans throughout the country joined the battle against the Plains tribes. They burned villages, destroyed crops, and killed bands of Indian hunters. Driven by hunger and fear, many Indians went to the reservations in South Dakota on their own. Others were rounded up and taken to the reservations. Once there, they had to turn over their weapons and horses to authorities.

Red Cloud and other chiefs, facing starvation, finally agreed to sign a treaty that gave away the Black Hills and the lands to the west to the federal government. In May

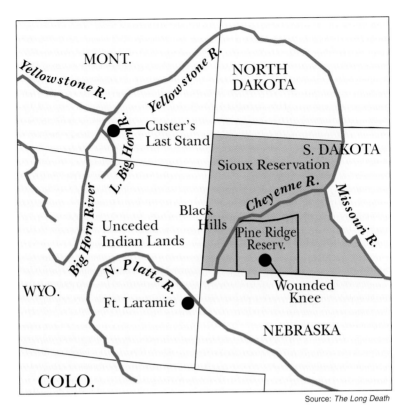

Hundreds of Americans and Indians lost their lives in battles over the lands surrounding the Black Hills.

1877, Crazy Horse led his weary warriors into Red Cloud's reservation, where the Indian leader surrendered to the U.S. army. Overcome by hunger and fatigue, the warriors could fight no more. A U.S. officer killed Crazy Horse in September 1877 as the Indian warrior was being taken to a Florida prison. Indian followers buried his body on the banks of Wounded Knee Creek.

Sitting Bull escaped with his forces to Canada. Eventually he turned himself in to Americans in North Dakota. After spending time in custody at Fort Randall, he was sent to live on a Sioux reservation in North Dakota. The fierce war chief later toured the country with Buffalo Bill's Wild West Show. Unrepentant, he portrayed himself as the Indian who conquered Custer's army.

DEATH OF A DREAM

The day-to-day life of Indians on the reservations was grim. With no place to hunt, the tribes had to rely on government handouts for food. In 1890, many Indians died when the government cut rations. During that time, a new religion called the Ghost Dance spread rapidly through the dispirited Plains tribes. Its followers danced to a fever pitch, sometimes for hours at a time. In the midst of the dance, exhausted dancers fainted. After regaining consciousness, they told of seeing a paradise where their dead relatives lived a joyful existence.

The large gatherings of Ghost Dancers, the Indians' passion for the religion, and their visions frightened American officials. Fearing the religion would incite the dancers to another rebellion, the agents decided to arrest Sitting Bull, whom they suspected of backing the Ghost Dancers. Indian police officers, paid by the federal government to maintain peace on the reservation, went to arrest the chief on December 15, 1890. When he resisted, he was killed.

Sitting Bull's murder drove the Ghost Dancers to seek protection from Big Foot, a Lakota chief whose village was on the Cheyenne River. Pursued by the army, the Ghost Dancers and Big Foot's band of men, women, and children headed for Pine Ridge, South Dakota, where

Red Cloud was now living. On December 29, 1890, the Seventh Cavalry surrounded them on the banks of Wounded Knee Creek. The soldiers began taking weapons from the Indians, who believed they would then be allowed to go to Red Cloud's reservation nearby.

Without warning, a single shot fired. An army officer had tried to wrest a gun from a deaf Indian who had not heard the order to surrender his weapon, and his gun had gone off accidentally. Already tense, cavalrymen began shooting into the crowd of Indians. Those who still had their weapons fired back, but they were no match for the army's artillery. Terrified women grabbed screaming children and tried to run through the line of firing soldiers to cover. At the end of twenty minutes, most of the small band lay dead. For the next hour, soldiers shot at anybody who moved. One hundred forty-six Indians died at Wounded Knee, their bodies covered with snow that fell the following night. For three days the stiff corpses lay on the lands of their ancestors; on the fourth day they were buried in a pit near Crazy Horse's grave.

The massacre ended the Ghost Dance and the hope of the Indian people to survive on their own terms. Black Elk, an Oglala Indian who witnessed the events at Wounded Knee, described what was lost:

> I can see that something else died there in the bloody mud, and was buried in the blizzard. A people's dream died there. It was a beautiful dream. . . . The nation's hoop is broken and scattered. There is no center any longer, and the sacred tree is dead.[9]

Tribes in the Southern Plains, California, and Oregon endured similar suffering. When Mexicans wrested control of their country from the Spaniards in 1821, they freed the Indians from missions in California, New Mexico, and Texas, where they had worked as virtual slaves. But the Mexicans also took over the tribal lands of the Indians, burned their villages, and left them with no choice but to work on Mexican ranches.

The few tribes that had eluded the Spanish lost their lands after the Mexican War opened the area to American settlers in the second half of the nineteenth century. Eventually, most either died or retreated to reservations. By 1900, only 10,000 to 20,000 California Indians survived. Their population, which had reached 310,000 in 1769, later increased during the twentieth century.

The Navajos, or Dinés, of Arizona and New Mexico had learned to herd sheep and farm from Spanish missionaries in the 1500s. When the United States conquered Mexico in the Mexican War of 1846–1848, settlers and the U.S. Army invaded the Navajo homelands. Under the leadership of Kit Carson, the army drove the tribe three hundred miles across the plains to a reservation in eastern New Mexico. Many died on the long hike during the winter of 1864.

At the reservation at Bosque Redondo, the Navajos had little food to eat and polluted water to drink. Thousands died before the government relented and allowed the desperate tribe to return to their homes. In 1868, Navajo leaders signed a treaty that set out the terms of

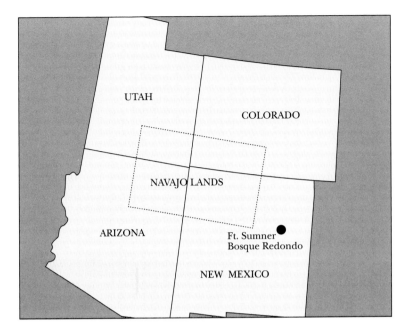

The Navajo tribe walked three hundred miles across the Southwestern plains to a reservation in eastern New Mexico.

their people's release. In exchange for their freedom, the tribe agreed to give up their weapons, not attack Americans, and send their children to American schools. As a result, the tribe still lives on ancestral lands and is today the largest Indian nation in the United States.

GRAVEYARD OF THE NORTHERN INDIAN

Farther north, the Nez Percé Indians lived a peaceful life, fishing for salmon, hunting game, and collecting wild foods in the mountains and streams of Washington, Oregon, and Idaho. The tribe, who had befriended the explorers on the Lewis and Clark expedition, had never battled with Americans. As homesteaders began to settle on their lands, tribal leaders signed a treaty on June 11, 1855. The treaty terms required the Indians to stay on a smaller area reserved for them and protected from trespassers. When gold was found on the Indians' reserve, a flood of adventurers poured into the region. These new trespassers, intent on making a fortune, ignored the terms of the treaty and threatened the peace.

At a conference held in 1863, government agents forced several Nez Percé chiefs to sign another treaty. Under the new treaty, signed June 9, 1863, the tribe lost six million acres of their land to settlers. Left with only a tenth of their original reserve, the Indians received 8¢ an acre for the ceded land.

Other Nez Percé chiefs, who had left the conference in disgust, protested that the treaty had not been approved by the tribe and was, therefore, not valid. Chief Hin-mah-too-yah-lat-kekht, also known as Chief Joseph, led his people in a six-year standoff with army troops sent to move the tribe to a tiny reservation in Idaho. Realizing, finally, that his people would lose against the forces of the U.S. Army, Chief Joseph led his tribe toward the reservation, where those who had signed the treaty lived. But a small band of young warriors, riled by the retreat, attacked and killed four settlers.

Chief Joseph knew the action meant war. After scoring a victory against the army at Whitebird Canyon, the band traveled more than one thousand miles across Wyoming and Montana to seek refuge in Canada. About fifty miles from the Canadian border, the group of 750 men, women, and children were surrounded by U.S. soldiers.

Chief Joseph surrendered on October 5, 1877, after many of his band were killed.

The army took the Nez Percé rebels to a reservation in eastern Kansas. Unused to the hot climate, many of the Nez Percé tribe died in the hot, swampy region that came to be known as the "graveyard of the northern Indian." By 1884, only 280 of the rebel group still lived. Chief Joseph lobbied the government to allow his people to join the rest of the tribe in Idaho. Finally, in 1885, the surviving members of the band joined other northern tribes—though not the Nez Percé Indians—in Washington Territory.

ALLOTMENT ACT

On February 8, 1887, Congress passed the Allotment Act, which ordered that lands owned by the tribes, including those on reservations, be divided among individual tribe members. Reformers supported the bill because they thought it would help Indians—as homesteaders—blend into American life faster. In fact, the Allotment system threatened tribal society. For centuries, tribe members had pooled their resources and worked as a group. By giving members their own plots of land, the Allotment Act undercut the sense of community.

The act also served to rob tribes of even more land. When the Department of the Interior allotted the land, each Indian received enough to set up a homestead, usually 160 acres. Leftover land went not to the tribe but to settlers and land speculators, who paid the tribe a small amount—sometimes as little as one-tenth of the value.

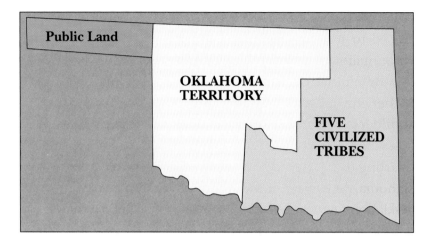

Members of the Five Civilized Tribes wanted to form their own state, to be called Sequoyah, in eastern Oklahoma.

Used to managing land as a tribe, individual Indians had no desire or know-how to farm a single plot of land. Many sold their tracts to settlers. As a result of the act, Indians throughout the country lost a total of ninety million acres of land from 1887 to 1933. That amounted to more than half the lands they controlled when the act was adopted.

OKLAHOMA RUN

Jostling to get the best place in line, families aboard covered wagons, men on foot, frontiersmen astride horses, and farmers riding mules waited impatiently for the Oklahoma Run to begin. Thousands of them had begun lining up along the Oklahoma border long before dawn. At exactly noon on April 22, 1889, a gunshot fired above the crowd. With a crack of the whip, they were off. They raced to stake claim to the land that lay beyond in the mountains, river valleys, and plains of central Oklahoma.

By nightfall, the beginnings of Oklahoma City and other towns appeared under the western sky. The builders joined other settlers—called Sooners because they had crept across the borders sooner than the legal starting date—on two million acres of land in central Oklahoma. As a result of the Allotment Act, most of western Oklahoma was opened to homesteaders. Before the end of the year, the western half of Indian Territory had become the Territory of Oklahoma.

The members of the relocated "Five Civilized Tribes" retained their lands in eastern Oklahoma, occupying twenty million acres. The five tribes formed their own government, and, in 1905, drew up a constitution for a proposed state they named Sequoyah. The members of the tribes met to discuss the matter at a constitutional convention at Muskogee on August 21, 1905. During heated debate, full-blooded Indians pressed to admit Sequoyah as a new state into the Union. Many of the half-white members, however, wanted the area to merge with the Territory of Oklahoma when it became a state. Their forces eventually won.

When Oklahoma entered the Union in 1907, Congress doled out portions of the eastern section among the individual Indians who lived there. The U.S. government sold the land left over to settlers. Again, thousands of prospective land owners gathered at the borders to race into Oklahoma to claim what was once Indian lands.

Militant Indians from the American Indian Movement took control of the town of Wounded Knee, South Dakota, in 1973, to protest their tribes' treatment by the U.S. government.

Seven

AFTERMATH

In the first decade of the twentieth century, only about 250,000 Indians survived in the United States. Starvation, disease, and attacks by U.S. troops wiped out entire tribes. Two and a half centuries of treaties had robbed tribes of their lands, their livelihood, and, in many cases, their lives. Recognizing the "great frauds and wrongs" committed on Indians under the guise of treaties, Congress passed a thirty-page appropriation bill on March 3, 1871, that banned further treaties with the Indians. The bill also decreed that tribes would not be considered independent nations. However, treaties already negotiated were to be honored.

Though designed to end treaty abuses, the bill caused further damage to Indians by eliminating their status as tribes. New appropriations bills enabled the federal government to divide tribal lands among individual Indians and then buy off the plots one by one. In this way, the government continued the policy of forcing Indians off lands

113

reserved for them and driving them to ever-smaller tracts of land. Cramped onto tiny reservations, the tribes could no longer practice their traditional ways of life and were reduced to depending on government rations to survive.

Even tribes in the wilderness of Alaska did not escape the land grab. They had lived for years on tribal lands and large reservations set up for them by the U.S. government. The Tongass Act, which went into effect on August 8, 1947, took millions of acres from the Alaskan tribes. Under the act, Alaskan landowners with two or more grandparents of Indian ancestry had to turn over land and timber to the United States. They received no payment for their property.

Members of Congress claimed that the Indian tribes who owned the land were incapable of developing it. The land, proponents argued, was a national resource that had to be developed for the good of America. Other supporters of the bill said that it was insulting to put Indians on reservations, where much of the land in question was located. Instead, they argued, Indians should be "freed" from reservations.

After heated debate, the Senate passed the controversial bill at 2 A.M. of the last day of the session. Felix S. Cohen, a lawyer who defended Indian claims, later noted that Indians had for years harvested timber and mined minerals more efficiently than had developers of public lands. Furthermore, he said, the tribes had a better conservation record.

"The chief justification for the present raid on Indian resources," said Cohen, "is therefore the high moral line that reservations and Federal protection of Indian lands

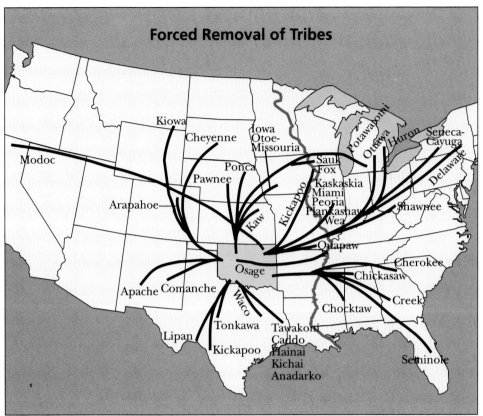

Forced Removal of Tribes

Kiowa
Cheyenne
Iowa
Otoe-Missouria
Modoc
Ponca
Pawnee
Sauk
Fox
Kaskaskia
Miami
Peoria
Piankashaw
Wea
Arapahoe
Kaw
Kickapoo
Potawatomi
Ottawa
Huron
Seneca-Cayuga
Delaware
Shawnee
Osage
Quapaw
Cherokee
Chickasaw
Apache
Comanche
Creek
Waco
Chocktaw
Tonkawa
Tawakoni
Caddo
Lipan
Kickapoo
Hainai
Kichai
Anadarko
Seminole

Sources: *Americans All* and *Compton's Encyclopedia*

Indian tribes from the East and the West were forced to move to Indian Territory in what would later become the state of Oklahoma.

are degrading. 'Emancipating the Indian' has become the catchword of those who would like to free the modern Red Man from his property."[1]

Congress did take some positive steps to help the tribes. After centuries of trying to force Indian tribes to adopt American ways, the United States government finally changed its course. In 1934, Congress passed the Indian Reorganization (Wheeler-Howard) Act, which recognized Indian tribes as separate entities. Under the law, tribes were once again allowed to run their own affairs. The act also stopped the division of tribal lands.

Congress attempted to further the cause of Indian rights when it passed the Act of August 13, 1946. The act established an Indian Claims Commission to settle claims brought by tribes against the United States. More than 170 tribes filed 370 complaints with the commission during the next thirty-two years. Until 1978 when it closed down, the commission awarded a total of $818 million to tribes.[2] Most of the money went to pay tribes for land taken by treaty at prices far below the fair value.

Unfortunately, many of the claims became tangled in legal red tape. In a typical case, the Sioux filed a complaint in August 1951 seeking to recover their losses as a result of the Treaty of Fort Laramie. The case took nearly eighteen years to settle. When the tribe finally received $1.6 million in the case, $350,000 went to lawyers and to pay expenses. Ultimately, the tribe got $315,000 to invest, and each of the thirty-six hundred members of the tribe received $262.[3]

In the 1950s, the government shifted course once again, this time focusing on relocating the Indians to cities and terminating the federal government's relationship with tribes. Between 1955 and 1957, almost ten thousand Indians left their reservations to work in cities.[4] In its efforts to reduce tribes' dependence on the federal government, Congress cut federal social services to the tribes, required them to pay taxes, and eliminated government loan programs. Under the new laws, tribes lost their special status as separate political groups. To cope with the overwhelming financial burdens, many of the tribes sold their holdings, and their members scattered.

During the 1960s and 1970s, young Indian activists took over buildings, blocked roads, and held demonstrations to protest the tribes' treatment. Their actions, including an armed confrontation with U.S. soldiers at Wounded Knee in 1973, made the American public more aware of the problems Indians faced. The protests also gave Indians a sense of pride and renewed interest among members in the old tribal ways.

The Indian Self-Determination and Education Act, passed by Congress in 1975, repealed the termination acts of the 1950s and put much of the responsibility of government reservations in the hands of the tribes. However, Indians on reservations still have to endure many regulations imposed on them by the Bureau of Indian Affairs.

Today, there are 287 Indian reservations, ranging in size from the sixteen-million-acre tract in New Mexico, Arizona, and Utah occupied by the Navajos to areas less than one hundred acres. More than half of the two million Indians now living in the United States reside in Oklahoma, California, Arizona, New Mexico, Alaska, and Washington. Though only about 22 percent live on reservations, many more return to tribal lands for special celebrations and religious rites.[5] As citizens of the United States, Indians can vote, own property, and live wherever they choose.

Since 1978, when the Claims Commission shut down, tribes have sought justice in U.S. courts, where Indians

117

have had mixed results. In response to a 1980 court case, Congress passed the Maine Indian Land Claims Settlement Act that gave Maine's Indians $81.5 million in trust fund money and timberland as payment for lands taken from them by the government during the last two centuries. Another court settlement gave twenty-five tribes in Washington state the right to 50 percent of the salmon caught each year in Puget Sound. Still other cases are pending.

Most of the tribal lands are gone, settled long ago by American settlers claiming divine rights to the fields, mountains, and rivers of a continent. Many tribe members have married Anglo-Americans, and their children have married Anglo-Americans. Hanging on the wall beside ancient Indian symbols are the relics of the Christian faith, brought to the tribes by determined missionaries.

Alcoholism, suicide, and hunger continue to haunt those living on the reservations. But despite centuries of abuse and hardship, of relentless efforts to make them American, the Indian nations persist. The tribes still practice their ancient rituals; the storytellers recite the oral histories of their people to the next generation. The people and their culture survive.

INTRODUCTION

1. Nabokov, Peter, ed., *Native American Testimony: A Chronicle of Indian-White Relations from Prophecy to the Present, 1492–1992* (New York: Viking, 1991), p. 118.
2. Josephy, Alvin M. Jr., *500 Nations: An Illustrated History of North American Indians* (New York: Alfred A. Knopf, 1994), p. 311.
3. Nabokov, p. 133.

CHAPTER ONE

1. Josephy, p. 211.
2. Billington, Ray Allen, *Westward Expansion: A History of the American Frontier* (New York: Macmillan Co., 1960), p. 74.
3. Josephy, p. 215.
4. Billington, p. 78.
5. Josephy, p. 217.

CHAPTER TWO

1. Peare, Catherine Owens, *William Penn: A Biography* (New York: J. B. Lippincott Co., 1956), 256.
2. Blumenthal, Walter Hart, *American Indians Dispossessed* (New York: Arno Press, 1975), p. 22.
3. Nammack, Georgiana C., *Fraud, Politics, and the Dispossession of the Indians* (Norman, Oklahoma: University of Oklahoma Press, 1969), p. 29.

4. Blumenthal, p. 16.
5. Josephy, p. 258.
6. Ibid., p. 256.
7. Ibid.
8. Ibid., p. 257.

CHAPTER THREE

1. Viola, Herman J., *After Columbus: The Smithsonian Chronicle of the North American Indians* (New York: Orion Books, 1990), p. 110.
2. Blumenthal, p. 52.
3. Viola, p. 118.
4. Ibid.
5. Blumental, p. 28.
6. Ibid., p. 27.
7. Ibid.
8. Adams, Henry, *History of the United States of America During the Administrations of Thomas Jefferson* (New York: The Library of America, 1986), p. 343.

CHAPTER FOUR

1. Adams, p. 346.
2. Blumenthal, p. 33.
3. Ibid.
4. Viola, p. 145.
5. Ibid., p. 129.
6. Billington, p. 275.
7. Adams, p. 353.
8. Ibid., p. 354.
9. Ibid., p. 356.
10. Ibid.

11. Josephy, p. 310.

12. Adams, p. 358.

13. Viola, p. 131.

14. Adams, p. 1197.

CHAPTER FIVE

1. Catlin, George, *Letters and Notes on the Manners, Customs, and Conditions of North American Indians, Volume II* (New York: Dover Publications, 1973), p. 211.

2. Ibid., p. 217.

3. Nammack, p. xv.

4. Viola, p. 135.

5. Ibid., p. 137.

6. Blumenthal, p. 71.

7. Ibid., p. 115.

8. Ibid., p. 94.

9. Ibid., p. 101.

10. Ibid., p. 98.

11. Ibid., p. 97.

12. Ibid., p. 102.

13. Ibid., p. 97.

14. Ibid., pp. 76–77.

15. Josephy, p. 327.

16. Blumenthal, pp. 69–70.

17. Ibid., p. 160.

18. Josephy, p. 328.

19. Blumenthal, p. 77.

20. Ibid., pp. 78–79.

21. Ibid., pp. 188–190.

22. Ibid., p. 82.

23. Ibid., p. 76.

24. Ibid.
25. Ibid., p. 81.
26. Ibid., p. 86.
27. Ibid., p. 84.
28. Catlin, pp. *n* 221–222.

CHAPTER SIX
1. Blumenthal, p. 85.
2. Ibid.
3. Ibid., p. 107.
4. Ibid., p. 62.
5. Josephy, p. 366.
6. Ibid., p. 389.
7. Andrist, Ralph K., *The Long Death: The Last Days of the Plains Indian.* (New York: Macmillan, 1964), p. 122.
8. Josephy, p. 402.
9. Josephy, p. 442.

CHAPTER SEVEN
1. Blumenthal, pp. 178–179.
2. Viola, p. 245.
3. Ibid.
4. Nabokov, p. 336.
5. *Information Please Almanac Atlas & Yearbook 1995* (New York: Houghton Mifflin Co., 1995), p. 674.

OTHER REFERENCES
Josephy, Alvin M. Jr., *The Patriot Chiefs: A Chronicle of American Indian Leadership.* (New York: Viking Press, 1961).

FURTHER READING

Andrist, Ralph K. *Long Death: The Last Days of the Plains Indians*. New York: Macmillan, 1964.

Baldwin, Louis. *Intruders Within: Pueblo Resistance to Spanish Rule and the Revolt of 1680*. Danbury, Conn.: Franklin Watts, 1995.

Brown, Dee. *Wounded Knee: An Indian History of the American West*. New York: Henry Holt, 1974.

Brown, Vinson. *Crazy Horse: Hoka Hey!*. New York: Benchmark Books (Marshall Cavendish Corp.), 1991.

Calloway, Colin G., ed. *The World Turned Upside Down: Indian Voices from Early America*. New York: Bedford Books of St. Martin's Press, 1994.

Force, Roland W., and Maryanne Tefft Force. *The American Indians*. New York: Chelsea, 1990.

Fritz, Jean. *The Double Life of Pocahontas*. New York: Benchmark Books (Marshall Cavendish Corp.), 1983.

Garbarino, Merwyn S. *The Seminole*. New York: Chelsea, 1988.

Goldman, Martin S. *Crazy Horse: War Chief of the Oglala Sioux*. Danbury, Conn.: Franklin Watts, 1996.

Golston, Sydele E. *Changing Woman of the Apache: Women's Lives in Past and Present*, Franklin Watts, Danbury, Conn., 1996.

Gravelle, Karen. *Soaring Spirits: Conversations with Native American Teenagers*. Danbury, Conn.: Franklin Watts, 1995.

Green, Michael A. *The Creeks*. New York: Chelsea, 1990.

Greenberg, Judith E. and Helen Carey McKeever. *A Pioneer Woman's Memoir*. Danbury, Conn.: Franklin Watts, 1995.

Hoig, Stan. *The Cheyenne*. New York: Chelsea, 1989.

Iverson, Peter. *The Navajos*. New York: Chelsea, 1990.

Josephy, Alvin M. Jr., *500 Nations: An Illustrated History of North American Indians*. New York: Alfred A. Knopf, 1994.

———. *The Indian Heritage of America*. Boston: Houghton Mifflin, 1991.

Meltzer, Milton. *Andrew Jackson And His America*. Danbury, Conn.: Franklin Watts, 1993.

Nabokov, Peter, ed., *Native American Testimony: A Chronicle of Indian-White Relations from Prophecy to the Present, 1492–1992*. New York: Viking, 1991.

Perdue, Theodore. *The Cherokee*. New York: Chelsea, 1988.

Press, Petra. *Multicultural Portrait of The Move West*. New York: Benchmark Books (Marshall Cavendish Corp.), 1995.

Thomas, David Hurst, et al. *The Native Americans*. Atlanta: Turner Publishing, 1993.

Viola, Herman J. *After Columbus: The Smithsonian Chronicle of the North American Indians*. New York: Orion Books, 1990.

Washburne, C. Kott. *Multicultural Portrait of Colonial Life*. New York: Benchmark Books (Marshall Cavendish Corp.), 1995.

INDEX